AF269327

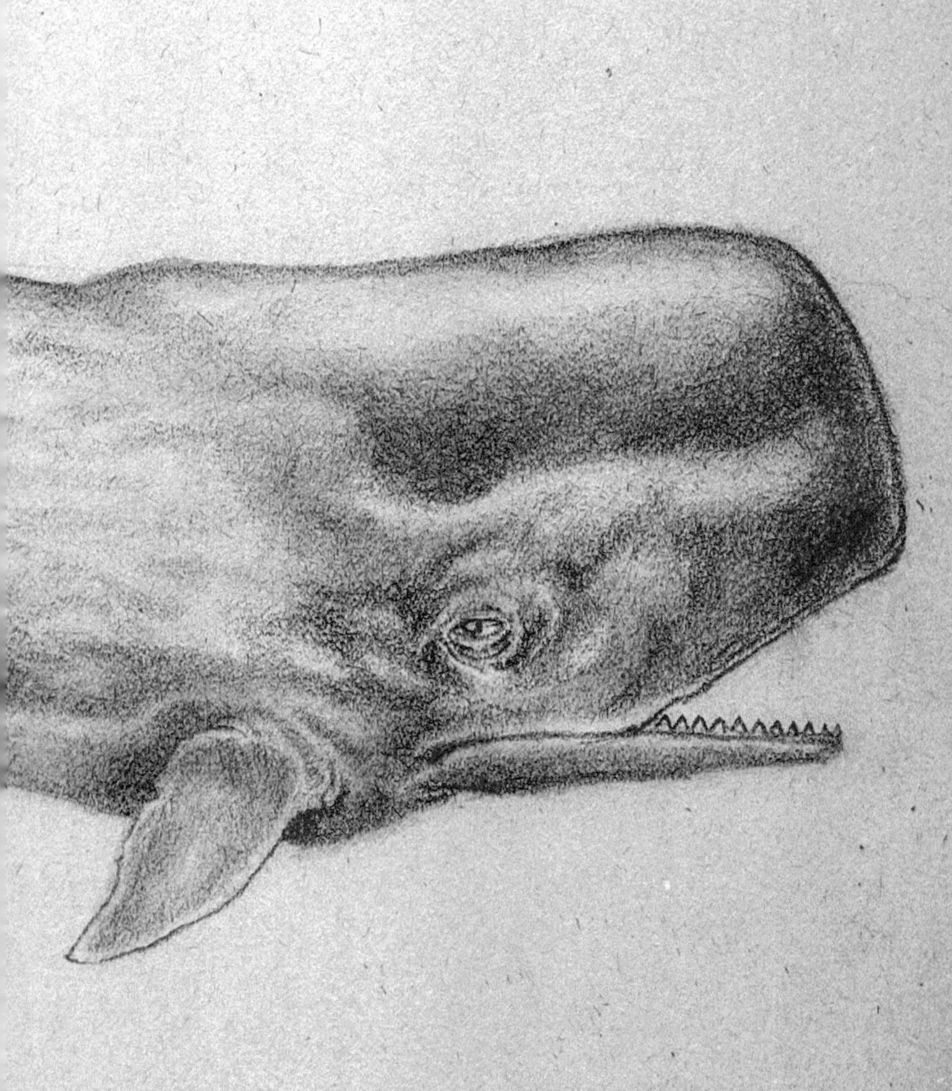

heck, texas

not a novel

tex gresham

ATLATL PRESS

Dayton, Ohio

2020

Atlatl Press
POB 521
Dayton, OH 45401
info@atlatlpress.com
www.atlatlpress.com

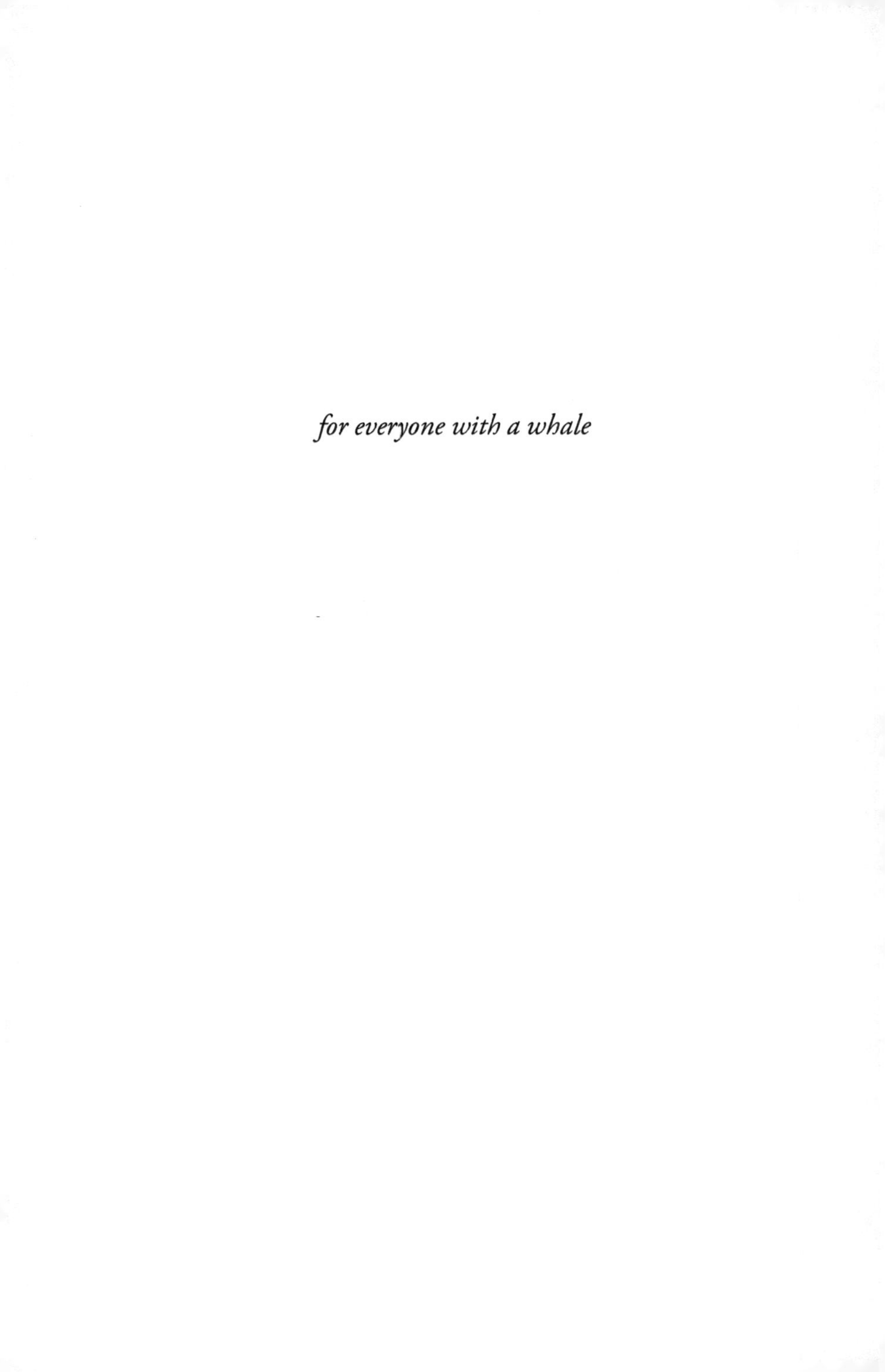

for everyone with a whale

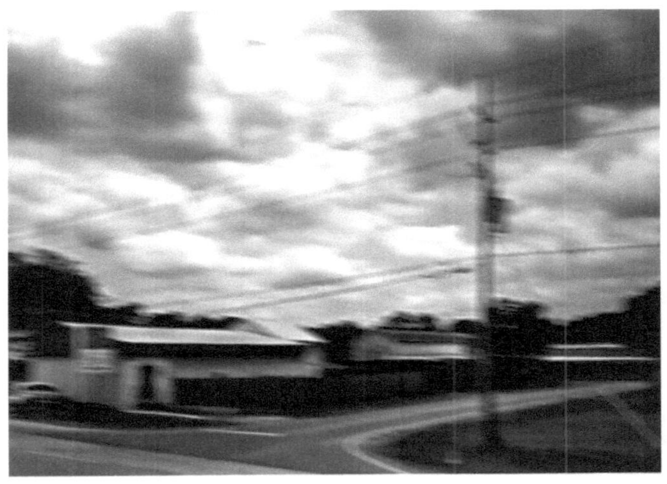

welcome to texas, fucker

1.

**these are the things that fall out of my
head as i lie in a ditch & die**

come one come all
the freakshow is the public
see the geek sucking the head off a cock
see the consumer's pain always on display

everyone's clothes fade eventually

there's a novel that no one reads and it starts with this thing about going grim about the mouth and wanting to knock people's hats off or some shit like that. if it weren't already in a book that's how i'd start this except i wouldn't say grim about the mouth and wanting to knock people's hats off. that's fucking lame. i'd say—

when i'm pissed and don't want to be myself but instead someone i know so that i can beat the shit out of him i like to take to the sea. no one hates me more than me.

It's written on a sign taped to a light post—kind of like one of those faded posters for missing dogs & cats, animals the owners know are already dead. The stop light swallows everything in a darkroom ambiance. He reads the sign again, wondering what it could mean, feeling the steering wheel vibrations of a car that's a decade overdue for a tuneup. A kick drum in the backseat rattles hollowly. He can smell the slaughterhouse a mile away.

He lifts his eye patch. He rubs at the empty socket and conceals his private eye. He takes a hit off a joint…out…and then the night takes on a Plasticine quality, an oil painting by an artist who is skillful in their conception but horrific in their execution: shadows & highlights incongruous enough to be labeled realistic surrealism; clouds too full, absorbing light that's too there, covering a moon that seems added in after the paint's dried. & someone's gone & spilled a 5-gallon bucket of clear acrylic over the whole thing, giving it all that creepy-plastic-couch-cover look—nothing can stain the velvet darkness. Nothing can clean the stains already there, now forever trapped.

The lights change—he drives.

**i am trying to ease you into life in jasper, texas
but really… fuck your comfort**

*At a bar. An Old Woman comes up to a Young Man & grabs his
cock.*

>OLD WOMAN: Fuck me?
>
>YOUNG MAN: Aren't you too old to be horny?
>
>OLD WOMAN: It still rains in the Sahara, honey.

today i saw twin brothers. white guys. standing in front
of a mirror at hot topic. they were trying on lil pump
shirts. the shirts were so big they looked like dresses.
the brothers were saying *we two fine ass bitches. we got
all the money. all the pussy.* they never bought anything.
what i was doing in hot topic is none of your business.

too tired to go to work, the man calls in sick. lying in bed, he is
unaware that the woman covering his shift has just learned she's got
colon cancer from holding in her shit all the time.

---

to continue with more shit like this, turn the page
to stop reading shit like this, burn the book

despite the ultrasound, i am certain my daughter will be born horribly deformed.

heredity will not be kind to her. she will get the worst of us.

but even if she comes out like this

i will still love her

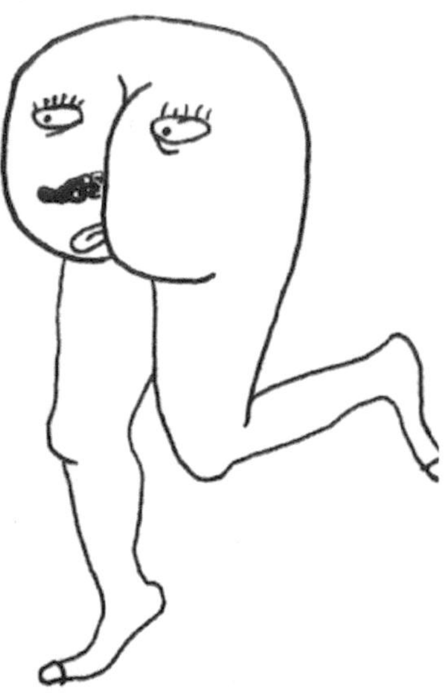

we ended up not having a daughter

she didn't make it long enough to be born

divorce is common in jasper, texas

HER: Your asking me about him and I'm telling you that there are things I don't want to talk about. Not because I can't, but because there are things better left not thought about. He is what he is. I asked him, begged him, explained to him all the ways he made me feel—not necessarily for him to change, but just to acknowledge and to adapt, to take my emotions into the same consideration he does his own—but, well, it's that whole falling on deaf ears thing with him. Like, he gets it, but he gets it for about 2 or 3 days and then it's back to the same. Once, for like 4 months, he was someone else. Like, he was someone who cared about my Being in more than a support kind of way—where he considered me an extension of his Self and not a secondary weight on his shoulders. He didn't get mad at the simple things I did. Simple things? Okay so like when I would say something, he'd tell me I was saying it wrong. Nothing I ever talked about was right or correct. Most things I said had to be amended and edited. And it legitimately got to a point where I wondered if there was something wrong with the way I spoke. I found myself apologizing almost every time I said anything. Especially about the baby. But he's dead now so I don't really want to talk about him.

WHAT HE WOULD'VE SAID: You're *

"Dab on him before you kill him."

This was something overheard at a Klan rally in the Wal-Mart parking lot in Tomball, Texas (1993).

This was the origin of the term *dab*.

Her dad drove her through Vidor, Texas. He said "God tore off the devil's horns and cast them deep in the earth. Buried them in a secret place. God took power away from the devil. The only way the devil can get that power back is if the people gift the horns back to the devil. God buried one of the devil's horns out here. These people are looking for it." She said "What about the other one?" He said "No one knows." She thinks the other horn is buried somewhere near Jasper where they live. Maybe under her elementary school. On the way out of town, he points to a sign that reads *Only whites allowed outside after dark*. This is mostly true.

after dark, i am in a club in jasper, texas

ME: What is a mind? What is a thought? What is perception? What is reality? What is real? What is a what? What *is?* These are stupid questions. The person who asks these questions on a consistent basis is avoiding the result of these questions—or rather the thing that created the question. They are so focused on trying to understand reality that they cannot admire the beauty. —No, that's not right. Too preachy and beatific. What it is is that real is *this* and *this* is real and any antagonizing debate toward that answer, while valid and at the right of the debater, is totally wrong and misplaced. It is the inability to accept that some questions are unanswerable, despite what a man of Constant Science might believe. Our contemplation toward life reality existence being or whatever you wish to call it should remain open and constant, but it should always be rooted in the present—both time and relative space—and of a nature that will serve or benefit that which is Real. How do we know what's real? We see, touch, taste, hear, smell. We fucking experience it. Is it still there when we turn around? Yes, it is. How do we know? Because other people see it too. But what if other people are just figments of my reality? First off, you aren't saying this. And second, don't be so narcissistic. Are our experiences the same? No. Do we see things in the same way—both emotionally and physically? No. These should be and are very simplistic question/answer systems we should constantly bring to the Here & Now Thought mentioned before. Is someone else's experience of experiences any less valid than mine? Fuck no and never. To think so is to be cruel and sadistic and alienate yourself from being a human being. Which, at its core, is a betrayal of the right and reason to be experiencing this reality. But what happens to us after we die? … Doesn't matter. Never did. Not for us to know. Is that cruel? Only if you make it. Because despite how much it scares you, hurts you, betrays any peace you might be able to achieve, despite you feeling like you—and only you—are in this situation, you are not. But that isn't a question to be asked, because it brings nothing to the present. … I don't know though. I mean, I could be wrong.

STRIPPER: Okay, but like do you want a lapdance or not?

They each had bombs to destroy them in perfect ways. / Her bomb came in orange / pill bottles. His father used / a strop to cast cross-marks / on his back. His bomb came / in the shape of expectation. / It destroyed him completely. / Before it melted him / down, his father's bomb / resembled a ghost, a *faggot kissed in Cleveland.* / Her bomb came in the shape of being / a human. His bomb came / in the shape of failure. / Their bomb had the shape / of freedom. Our bomb came / in the shape of progress. And in perfect ways, / these bombs exploded / with terrible magic. The victims tripped / into a silence, silver and peaceful. / And those who still held / their bombs said goodnight / and secretly wished / for their countdown clocks to tick / twice as fast.

don't be fooled: anyone who tells a story that begins with *One time my friend* is really telling a story about themself that they don't want others to know is about them.

Remember how his breath smelled on the car ride from San Antonio to Jasper. The crust in his soul patch, you knew what that was. You'd walked in on him, knees to carpet, two men in his mouth, a glazed-ness to his face you've come to recognize as his heroin mask. It is your birthday and you were supposed to meet your girlfriend for dinner. But instead you've carried this marionette that used to be your friend, half-naked & stoned, to your car and now you're driving without any idea of where you're driving to. In three years you will hold the urn that holds his ashes and think about the way he fell into your arms when he thought you were there to save him.

When I was a kid my dad told me about a guy he saw eating spaghetti. The man's nose was so long that he had to lift it up to put the spaghetti in his mouth. I've been looking for this man for thirty years.

I had a dog growing up & it hated when I blew in its face. My mom would tell me it's b/c it was locked in a room with a fan when it was a puppy. This dog died. When its legs stopped working I would tie a rope around its back & lift it so that it could go pee & poop. My mom couldn't put it to sleep. So it died. Yesterday on the phone with my mom I mentioned the locked in the closet with a fan thing. She said *That's just something I told you so you'd stop blowing on the dog*. But she never told me anything to get me to stop french kissing the dog. This is probably why my sister & I don't talk anymore.

Showdown At Spark's Saloon in Jasper, Texas

Barry shoots Tough Guy Allen in the jaw & neck & while Tough Guy's all stumbling around & everything, grabbing at his neck to keep the blood in, Barry shoots Tough Guy above the eye. & then Tough Guy's dead. Lily—that hooker with the heart of gold, the one who tried to swallow acid & melted her lips off—just stands there & watches this. She used to work for Tough Guy Allen & he'd beat up on her daily. Barry has always loved Lily. She feels a love for Barry but not The Love. Not the Love that Barry dreams about whenever he can sleep. Barry set it all up so that Tough Guy & Lily are here—Tough Guy shot up & dead & Lily standing over his body saying *You shot him dead.* Barry wants to say *It's so that he never comes back, never hurts you again* but Barry's choking on the shot of vodka he's just taken. The one that's burning a little too much. He coughs & blood splatters the ground near Tough Guy's feet. Barry falls, swallowing blood, gasping for air that's stuck in his mouth. Lily leaves the bar with the money Barry's got stashed in the floor safe. She sets the money & herself on fire on the steps of the Morrison Public Library. This has never been made into a movie starring Johnny Depp.

The Sequel

An hour & forty-eight minutes of out-of-focus slaughter-house footage montaged to "Rosanna" by Toto—which has been pitched & stretched to an hour & thirty-nine minutes. The last nine minutes are silent so that the audience hears their own tinnitus. The final shot is a single frame closeup of the mole on Kathy Bates's left calf. The shot lasts six minutes & seventeen seconds & slowly pushes in on the mole until the screen is a near-black shade of melanomic brown. The end.

this is in the back of his car—kick drum with torn head, empty pack of newports, nine unused spiral notebooks, book about the coulthurst murders in alaska, & a gallon of eggnog.

coming up after the commercial break

at ty's diner a white man holds the door open for a latina in a purple dress. her husband, a tall black man who once played for a triple-a baseball team, turns to the white man and says *that's mighty white of you.* the couple's passing through town. the white man lives here. will they make it out alive?

if you can read the title *moby dick* and not giggle a little, you've died inside.

the hollywood drama ends like this

He can hear her screaming in the delivery room.
The labor is grit and high contrast.
Bleached out footage.
The nurse gives him a look—*not good.*
No idea this would happen.
Fade to black.
A child's voice: *Daddy.*
Fade in on—
Living room.
He's sitting in a chair imprinted with his legacy.
Lighting is precious metal, diffused.
Shot on warm film stock.
Wife's there, at the front door.
Then daughter, now seven—eight.
He says: *Did you have a good day at gymnastics?*
Daughter hugs him, sits in his lap.
Focus pulls them together.
Wife goes to the kitchen.
Close up: his face.
Daughter talks.
Slowly pull back.
Daughter's voice fades, echoes.
Sounds reverberate, a well-rehearsed nightmare.
Image drains to sterile light, steely color.
Decomposed film stock.
Slow pull back reveals he's still in the hospital.
In his wife's room.
Sitting in a chair imprinted in his memory.
Waiting for the empty bed to not be.
Waiting for the nurses to tell him to leave.
Cut to black silence.

there was a kid @ the junior high who shot himself in the head with a .22 in the first floor bathroom. it didn't kill him so he went up to the second floor bathroom and shot himself six more times in the head. He bled to ~~death~~ death. He wrote "oops" in his blood. his brother tried to shoot himself later that night in the treehouse the two had built as kids. Their father stopped him. But the gun went off. it was a shotgun. It blew the front of his face into mush. He works at the gas station by my house. He looks like this→ He talks like Sylvester the cat from the looney tunes.

THIS DIDN'T GET HIM A JOB

On the road, solitude is inevitable. Isolation, however, is optional—and a must. For this trip, I would like to use the American Southwest, the arid regions of Nevada along Route 50, the ghost towns it cuts through, and vast expanses of nothingness in between to attempt to touch upon the idea of isolation in America. What does it mean to be lonely? What can one do with loneliness? And what happens to nature and communities that live comfortably in isolation? Part road-trip narrative, part combo cartographic/historiographic documentation of landmarks and towns along Route 50, part pseudo-philosophical discussion of the meaning of loneliness. The project would culminate in—aside from the Instagram posts and the 300- to 500-word daily recap—a written narrative of the journey along Route 50, accompanied by photos and sketches, and punctuated between days with short vignettes (around 5-10 mins) about each day. I'm good enough. Please give me this. I need it. I need to get out of here. I need to know I'm worth something better than this. I am in a quenchless feud with myself to prove that I am not cursed. I don't want to see the same things over and over again. I can't watch my parents die. I can't watch people trying to act happy. I can't watch the hate and the pain and the hell. I can't. Please. I need this.

THIS IS WHY HE WENT MISSING

IF YOU SEE HIM, PLEASE CALL ME

he might already be a ghost

at the secret lesbian bar in jasper, texas

                    WOMAN
Do you ever think about the shit we did?

                    GOTH
We?

                    WOMAN
People… like killing the dodo bird…

                    GOTH
The dodo bird?

                    WOMAN
We killed it. But like what if in its DNA
there was some unknown protein strand
that's got the cure for cancer or a way to
live forever or something.

                    GOTH
The dodo bird?

                    WOMAN
And we killed it.

                    GOTH
You're—

                    WOMAN
What… Oh… What if it was done on
purpose? What if the same force that's
keeping me on this path killed the
dodo, if only to keep… to prevent us
from… surviving.

                    GOTH
You're fucking nuts. That's a friend
telling you this.

                    WOMAN
Did you know that on his deathbed, as
he shuffled off this mortal coil, a fart
slipped from William Shakespeare's
mortal coil?

                    GOTH
Whatever was between us is extinct.

A CPA at a waste management facility in Jasper, Texas is let go from a company he's been with for 25 years. They give him a severance package and tell him that he can work through the month—and that if he does so they will give him a good recommendation. Three weeks later he brings with him a dual hot plate, two large skillets, a spatula, pancake mix, eggs, milk, butter, and a squirt bottle filled with partially-melted coconut oil. On this last day he treats all his coworkers to his "famous pancakes." Everyone gets one, some get two. Throughout the office he hears some *mmm*s and *wow*s and *these are surprisingly good* and even a *seeing as how no one's dead, I guess he didn't poison them*. A woman of about thirty who's just starting at the company asks *How do you get them so thick?* Everyone waits for him to answer. *It's the coconut oil* he says, shaking the squirt bottle full of his cum. His name is Chris. His phone number is ▮▮▮▮▮▮▮▮▮. This is mostly true.

i'm sure there are people out there who shrieked when they heard merle haggard died. screamed harder than they will when their parents die or if one of their children dies suddenly. i'm sure there are people out there who put all their emotions into merle haggard. cassette tapes on sale—buy one get two free.

everyone who lives in this goddamn town looks to the media for god. i think some people here found it in merle haggard. or maybe i'm thinking of david allan coe. but he's still alive.

when my mother-in-law used to visit, she would sleep on planks of wood & cinder blocks in the garage.

[cliché white girl name]

They all said she was a hard nut to crack. Little did they know her last name was Macadamia.

She asked her friend if she wanted to get shitfaced. When her friend said yes, she threw a bunch of shit in her face.

Not knowing she had Fuchs' Dystrophy, despaired by her declining vision, she took a fork to both of her eyes.

She was deposited six blocks from the event, wired to the active device, and was told to eliminate the target.

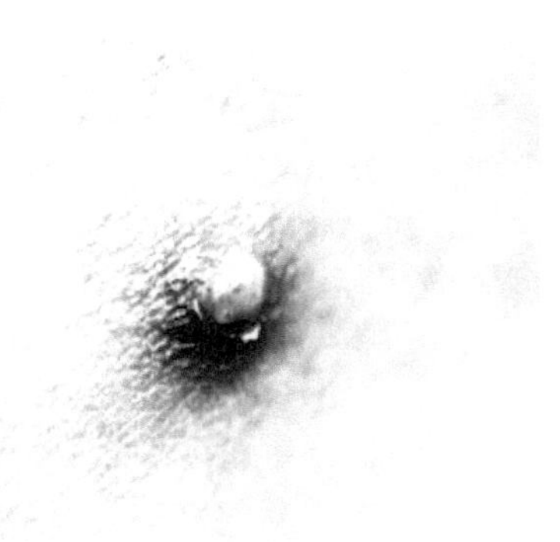

i thought this thing was a nipple
growing out of my chin but it was
the biggest pimple i've ever had & i
went in for a job interview w/ this
zit on my chin & i never got a call
back so i took a razor blade to it &
ended up in the hospital cuz while
i was trying to cut the pimple my
hand slipped & i cut both my wrists

i want to strike out and hunt down the horror, kill the fuck out of it—i would say it's to save anyone else from dying the way i have but it's a selfish thing: i want to fucking kill it. end it. put an end to it. sail across oceans of self-hate through storms charged by annihilation armed only with a set of spears dulled by how much i've jerked them off.

but there isn't some thing, one thing i can point to and wail "there she blows." no white whale.

unless you count my father.

or myself.

Dear Son,

Are you prepared for your heart to break? Are you prepared to find out that after all this time you actually have a heart that can break? Are you prepared to find out that the heart is much more than just a mass of tissue in the center of your chest that pushes blood through an intricate system buried under seven layers of skin? Are you prepared to understand that you cannot control how much the person you love loves you back because they too have a heart that may be uncontrollably connected to someone else, who isn't you, and the only thing you can do is let your heart beat and beat, and ache, and swell, and throb for them until the pain eventually subsides to a point that's just bearable and you can live a day without thinking of that someone, until, and this may never happen, until your heart begins to beat for someone else or for only yourself and it aches in new, almost-pleasurable but unidentifiably painful ways? Are you prepared to finally be over that other heart, yours no longer aching like it once did, but then you see them out there with someone that isn't you and they seem infinitely better than they ever did with you because they are doing things that you never did together because you didn't have the money or time, and so here they are, out with that someone who isn't you doing that thing that you never did and what you're seeing is a life that could've been yours but never will, and so when you see this that ache comes in suddenly, a pipebomb in your soul and every inch, not just your heart, feels pumped with shrapnel, that it's been dragged through all the Hell you can't imagine, and every microfiber of your being frays up and unravels and that pain brings with it a rationalization that the only way out of this pain, misery, overall Hell is death and that Death is falling on you like a monster and your world, your entire fucking life is over, fucked, fucking worthless and all you want is for death to hurry the fuck up and get here because you are far too chickenshit to be your own death? Are you prepared for all this? No? Then don't ever have a son.

Always,
Your Father

every two minutes someone dies from something you've never heard of.

including bullshit poisoning.

HOT COFFEE

cyanide in the percolator.

oily beans ground with human bone.

acid brought to a boil. let it drip.

steamed cum and cancerous raspberry sweetener.

blow the surface. careful, it's hot. sip.

work around in mouth. swallow.

unless it's too hot. then spit.

there are lines that go *all that most maddens cakes the brain & all the subtle demonisms of life & thought* and i like how they go & wish i would've thought of them first because this self-stabbing madness cakes the brain & these little demons, the pig-shaped ones, are all life & all thought.

She'd seen it on TV and wanted to see if it really worked. She wanted to see if she could do it too. The police had a difficult time collecting the pieces of her body. Her parents couldn't identify her face, so the coroner used her teeth. There was a moment of silence at her school. Some of the kids made jokes. The boy who'd taken her virginity cried on the floor of the girl's restroom clutching a pair of her panties. And nothing changed. A week later a boy in the next town over saw something on TV. He wanted to see if it really worked. He wanted to see if he could do it too.

There was a man in His house. A man with broken hands and a burnt heart and a spaghetti nose. It was dark and the man stood in a place He couldn't see. But He knew the man was there. He wanted to say *Get out*. All that came out was *Stay*. **And the man did. Forever. Amen.**

jesus cast demons into swine and the swine leapt to their deaths.
this is why bacon tastes so good.
it's a sin.

conversation between a pimp & his main piece in jasper, texas

"Baby… Baby, forget his ass. He's the type of clowndog who eats his salad first."

"He would only flatback with me."

"See. Salad first."

**at the brookshire brothers gas station near w. church &
holy ave. in livingston, tx:**

*Two drunk girls outside. Dancing to trap music coming from the
open trunk of a lowrider.*

SAMANTHA: I am alive, mother fuckers!
FERN: I am never having kids!

*There's a drunk frat boy wearing a Texas A&M hat hunched over
the trunk of an old Honda Accord. Head in his folded arms.*

FRAT BOY: Shut up!

*His hat slides off his head. Lands in a puddle of oil. Girls ignore
him. They slap their asses and grind on each other. Frat Boy's
friend comes out and lobs a bag of chips at his drunk friend. They
hit Frat Boy's head and land next to his hat in the oil.*

FERN: Hey! Sir!
ME: What?
FERN: Say yes!
ME: Yes.

**i often wake screaming about the finality of
death. it doesn't help that everyone has to
die. i don't give a shit about other people.**

**an arsonist burned down a house. a woman was inside and
she burned too. the police caught him a week later. this is
part of their conversation at the station in vidor, texas**

"There's this faggot who comes to the tractor shop. A goddamn
fucking clowndog. He wears a shirt that says *I'm an uncommon
human being* when I could go outside right now & piss on
someone just like him in about six seconds. It'd take longer
for me to put on my shoes. I think he walks around with a
finger in his asshole more than he doesn't. I guess that's kind
of uncommon. He's the kind of guy who makes buttfuck jokes
at a funeral for someone who died of colon cancer. He drives
a motorcycle. He paid $200 for tickets to see Whitesnake at
Grand Casino Coushatta in Louisiana & said they were *dope*."

"Aren't you supposed to ask me why I burned down the house?"

"Nah, you're free to go. That burned bitch was Mexican, so
who cares."

"Dope."

She lives in a house with twelve rat traps in each room. Every day there's a loud snap & one less rat. At the end of the week she sweeps up all the full traps into a dustpan the size of a small trash can & tosses the rats in a swamp behind the house—feed

the gators & vultures. Sometimes the snap is followed by the squeal of a rat with it's broken neck or shattered head pinched in the trap—unable to die. She takes a monkey wrench from the garage & crushes their

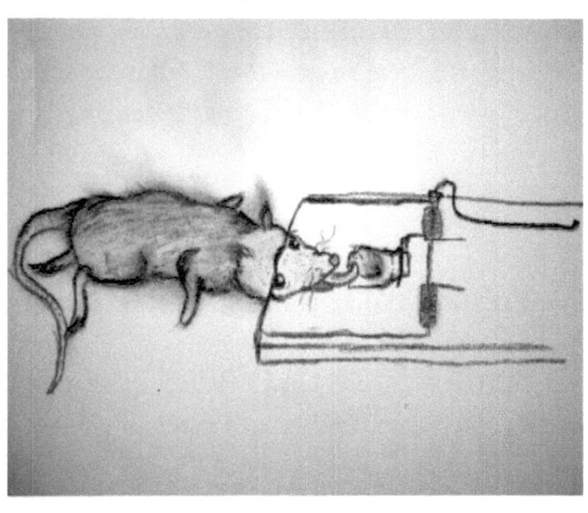

heads. She once cooked a pot pie in the oven. When it was done, she opened the oven & found it half-eaten. A rat burnt crispy sticking out of the pie. There are people who believe in the existence of secret societies that gather multiple times a year to enjoy cannibalism—almost never on small children, but sometimes. There are countries that eat deep fried cat, cats roasted on open spits. Homeless people cook cats in the swamp behind her house.

they chew through her walls

the thoughts of 96% of the population in vidor, texas

well, goddammit, if y'all didn't act like animals this shit wouldn't happen. i'm not acting like a part of the animal kingdom. all this whiteness striking out into the world is not of an ape or whale or worm. i'm not an animal. but you are acting like a savage. like an animal. we wouldn't have to kill you if you'd start acting like a human and not an animal. get off the floor of the animal kingdom and act civilized. maybe then we'll stop wanting to punish you, rub your nose in the shit you've made yourself.

overheard outside the taco bell in jasper, texas

12 YEAR WHITE OLD BOY: "Hell yeah I'd wipe my ass with a taco and feed it to a bitch if she stole my pizza."

at paradise trailer park in jasper, texas

Barry says, "Man, don't put furniture out on the side of the road. That's trashy. It's what lazy poor people do when they can't figure out how to get rid of something."

There's a woman in high heels, popping her ass up & down. She's too big for heels. Tall & chubby. She's on the verge of falling over. There's a couch on fire behind her.

Barry says, "That's one way to handle it."

He suffers from reality sickness.

She suffers.

Your favorite brand of disease
is back in stock

The roach crawled toward him, dragging its entrails like a forgotten fetus still clinging to the womb. Its movements were labored, shaking. What horror, he thought as he leaned his face closer to the roach. His hands went to the sides of his face. He wanted to scream as the roach crawled closer. He saw himself on the floor. He was the roach. He wanted to know how it tasted.

His teeth should be neatly arranged, but they aren't.

"I wore this shirt down on 6th street and everyone was like HEY YOU ASSHOLE!"
"Why would they call you an asshole?"
"Eh, I wouldn't pay a $10 cover to drink."

I linger, thinking there's more to add to all this. There isn't. Sometimes I like to pretend I'm shooting people as I pass them on the freeway. Whatever.

YOUNG BOY: I can't tell if it's sad or endearing, but I see my family as *The Simpsons.*

THERAPIST: Does your father choke you?

YOUNG BOY: No.

THERAPIST: Then why *The Simpsons?*

YOUNG BOY: Because we all have jaundice.

A daughter asks her father: *Daddy, is it fair to be alive when others are dead?* The father picks at a scab on his neck and says: *Yes. It's the fairest thing there is.* Later, when the girl is a woman and the father is a marble plaque in a manicured lawn, the girl won't think it's fair.

$$\frac{\text{art is}}{\text{rated}} \text{ seriously}$$

art is
seriously
————
rated

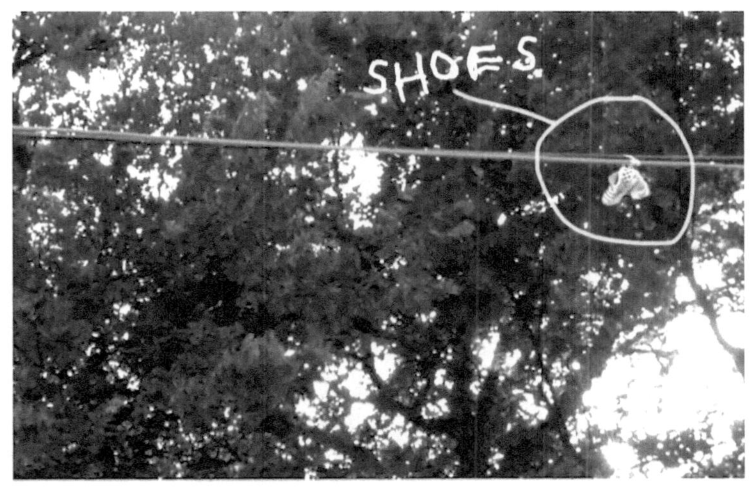

children grow up knowing that this means a meth house is near.
some children have sleepovers at these houses.
after the kids go to sleep, the parents get high
and swing at each other with cleavers.
they make eggs and bacon the next morning, still high.
they never mistake the sea salt for more meth.
but sometimes they mistake the meth for sea salt.

How the Showdown At Spark's Saloon in Jasper, Texas Really Went

Barry shoots Tough Guy Allen, except his name is just Allen. He's the foreman at the lumber factory where Barry works. Allen doesn't hit Lily & Lily isn't a prostitute. She rides a stool every night at the Redling Bar. Allen tries to get her to sleep with him. Barry is a jealous man. Lily likes this. Barry wants Lily to himself. Lily wants anyone. When Barry shoots Allen in the neck & gut & cock, Allen stumbles & tries to say *Forgive me God* but he hits the ground & dies. Lily says *Wow, you're so sweet* & gives Barry a kiss. They fuck & marry & have six kids in six years. One of these kids is my father. This is the basis for the movie *Yankee Doodle Daddy* starring Johnny Depp & Fran Drescher & Brendan Fraser, directed by Roman Polanski.

Current Rotten Tomatoes score: 84%

a mostly true conversation at Spark's Saloon

It's a double wide trailer that's repurposed into a bar. The owner's name is Stubb. He cooks a terrible steak and sleeps in a closet in the back. Two stool jockeys drink beer and stare at the TV. They talk to each other out the side of their mouths.

"Look, the only thing I deepthroat is a bottle of beer."
"I believe it."
"You know that song… Piano Man."
"Elton John."
"Nah, that other faggot."
"Billy Joel."
"Yeah. He was makin love to his tonic and gin so I could deep throat this American beer."
"Amen."

word around the swamp

Somebody had poisoned the dog food. When all the hobos ate it, most got sick. A few of the older ones died. The ones that survived got together to figure out who had poisoned them. Every time they tried to investigate anything, they'd all end up getting stoned or drunk. They uncovered nothing. They continued to eat the same brand of dog food and die.

things i didn't want to write out here in the ditch

—He sits alone at a table, TV set up across the room playing a VHS of a family Christmas—a VHS tape he found at a garage sale—and he eats dinner in the company of a family that isn't his.

—She drives a golf cart to the bakery daily to buy blueberry scones because they say she's too retarded to drive a car.

—I'm having to look up all the "big" words I used (even though I know them) because I have a feeling someone is going to quiz me.

—Did you hear the sound it made when the car fatally embraced your son?

—Babo shoots ten people at a gas station then turns the gun on himself. Tries to shoot his heart. Ends up paralyzing himself. Did you know they send cripples to the gas chamber? Whatever happened to the electric chair?

—One time my friend, uh, Starbuck was stalked by a mostly retarded girl @ our high school. She'd grab her pussy & thrust it at him. We'd laugh & *What the fuck?* our way into the next moment. Years later he told me he'd fucked her behind the out buildings during 4th period. She'd bled all over his pants. He said she moaned & thrust like a real girl. He said fucking her was a gift He said it was the nicest thing anyone will ever do for her.

i can't stop believing that all these cursed
moments infected me during a time when
i was too young & weak to defend myself
from their harm. people call it childhood,
look back on it warmly. i call it the Age of
Suffering & say nostalgia is poison. i pray
for the kids who are in that age. some escape.
some never find a way out of the labyrinth
but still move through the dark. some spear
themselves to that suffering & sink. maybe
i can help you. maybe i can sacrifice myself
for the children. the little piggies that go
oink oink in the freakshow inside my head.

2.

god doesn't love children
who dream of killing their parents

in a classroom at jasper high school

STUDENT: I didn't think spiders would live in the sun.

TEACHER: Of course they do. They're cold-blooded.

STUDENT: I didn't know they were cold-blooded. I thought they
were no-blooded.

TEACHER: What kind of animal on this earth do you know of
that is no-blooded?

STUDENT: Birds?

TEACHER: Get the fuck out of my classroom.

they think it's because she walked in her sleep but she'd
never done this before. toddlers don't sleepwalk. but it
was in the middle of the night that she walked out of the
house. her mother and her mother's boyfriend were in the
kitchen swinging at each other with cleavers so they didn't
hear the door open. it started snowing. she got lost in the
woods by her house. she got tired and sat on a rock. she fell
asleep. the police found her two days later. frozen all the
way through. they had to thaw her under the same lamps
they use to keep pizzas warm. they did an autopsy. there
was meth in her system.

jokes most often told in jasper, texas:

1) you hear about the jamaican guy who got prescribed zoloft?
doctor said he was suffering from a tropical depression.

2) what kind of animal do you get when you mix the intelligence of a dog and the attitude of a cat?
a woman.

3) a black guy & a mexican guy are in a cop car. who's driving?
the cop.

4) how do you get a bear to stop attacking you?
shave your chest and lose some weight.

5) **[CENSORED]**

6) how do you get a fag to fuck a woman?
shove a bunch of shit up her cunt.[1]

7) what's black, white, and red all over?
my wife after she lost the tv remote. ...stupid bitch.[2]

---

[1]   This is the priest's favorite.
[2]   This is the sheriff's favorite.

don't forget the offertory

The pain in her back grew more each morning. A throb following the pace of her heart. A lump causing stiffness in her spine. When she could no longer bear it, she visited her doctor. He poked and checked her, causing her more discomfort. He ordered an x-ray. When the results came back, his face was a whole graveyard. He told her *There's no easy way to put this, but you're pregnant. The pain you're feeling is a result of your ovaries and uterus being intertwined with your spine in a way I've never seen.* She said *But what does that mean? I haven't had sex in over a year.* He tells her that if her child continues to grow, the pressure against her spine will sever all nervous system functions, resulting in paralysis and possibly death. *You do have options* he said to her. She knew what that meant.

—Jump ahead, change perspective, ride the genetics of the mother, follow now the impossible daughter—

As she changes the cushion of her mother's wheelchair, Lucy waits. Her mama's got the knife in her hand, using what little strength she has to cut the cake. She knows her mama won't react like mamas are supposed to. Her mama's never seen her as a women—always a baby. The knife makes an incision down the all-white frosting, exposing the pink-tinted batter. Lucy says *It's going to be a girl.* She doesn't tell her mama that it's Ty's. Or might be, considering they haven't had sex yet. She doesn't need to tell her mama anything. The look her mama gives her scares her.

i'll cut off my fuckin leg. it's just meat.

i am both the hunter & the great white demon.

i am madness maddened.

i am pepperoni pizza face.

$5 hot-n-ready trash.

fuck little ceasars.

He hears that she was part of a gangbang at an undisclosed location in Houston. Not a grungy, dimly-lit room orgy with a bunch of fat guys jerking off over her half-doped attempts at pleasuring herself. He hears that it's an elite gathering, that she's paid well, that they all treat her nice—as nicely as one can be treated while getting their face plastered with cum. He even hears that she took two men at once. He's heard that she died at one of these events, snorted a line of something that cut her heart into unmanagable pieces.

who is this about?
    a) his ex-wife
    b) his daughter
    c) his mother

have you ever thought about this?
if wine is the blood of christ, then jesus must've been a fruit.
    a) yes
    b) no
    c) all hail satan

    one time my friend killed himself.
        a) this
        b) really
        c) happened

a white guy approaches a black guy in the back of a food town parking lot in jasper, texas

WHITE GUY: I like your shirt.

BLACK GUY: Listen, man: I appreciate your compliment. Sometimes when white people say nice things to me, as few & far between as that may be, it catches me off guard & I have trouble coming up with a reply. I'm treated by white people like a reject of humanity that it's hard to be connected to a white person such as yourself. So I just want to tell you I appreciate you as a person, for being a person, and for acknowledging me. Not that I need it, but sometimes I just lose hope that there will ever be any street-level civility between blacks and whites. We don't need each other to validate our existences, but we do need to validate each other's existence.

WHITE GUY: Great. Now gimme your fuckin wallet before I bust your head open.

zit photo

this is supposed to be a photo of a bad zit i have but i can't take a picture of it & when i tried to find one online i had to buy it & a stock photo of a zit that looks like mine is $75 so you'll have to use your imagination but to help you i'll say that the zit is massive & white & i can't get rid of it & when i was out in public today a little girl saw it & started crying & i wanted to rip it from my face but it is part of me & if i get rid of it then i won't have anything to blame my self-hate on & would have to accept that the ease with which i hate myself doesn't have to do with these pimples i hunt & exact revenge on but is instead solely my own terrible depression.

or something like that.

a piece of paper taped to the girls bathroom wall in jasper elementary in jasper, texas

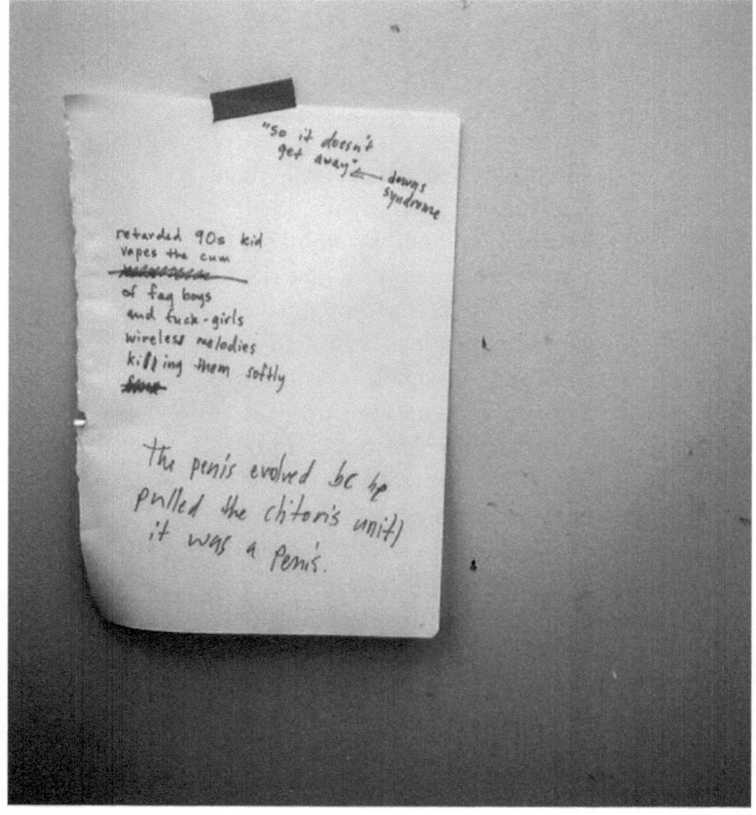

mostly true story

He wouldn't let the dog sleep inside so he tied its leash to a mesquite bush and went inside for the night. The deer lease walls were old and thin. The girl he'd taken could hear the coyotes tear apart the dog's skin and muscle. It screamed once and then didn't. She never forgave the man who'd taken her. He had killed her only friend in this world. In the morning there was nothing left but the collar and some fur. *It never felt a thing* said the man who'd taken her. She thought *But what about me?*

He bagged himself a twelve pointer. He dressed it in front of her, cutting up the middle, guts spilling out like groceries from a cheap plastic bag. He hung the carcass from a tree, pulling it high so the coyotes wouldn't get at it. That night, when he was asleep, the girl he'd taken snuck out to cut the rope so that the coyotes would eat what he cared about most. He never heard a thing. He stepped out the next morning and saw a shred of pink fabric from her shirt. It was all that was left.

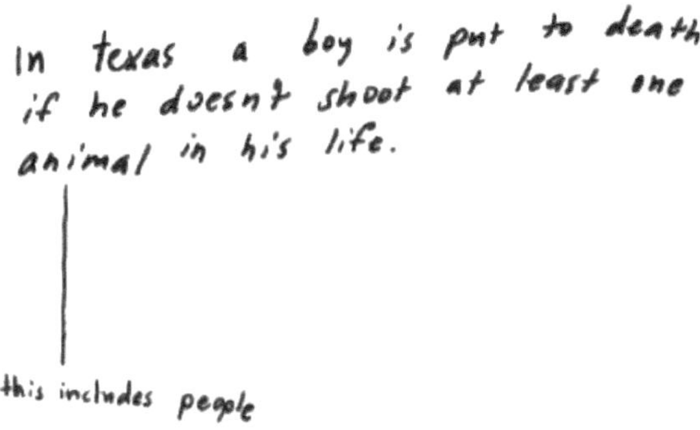

in the faculty lounge at jasper high school

COACH: I don't like vaginas. They stink like old lunch meat.

TEACHER: No way, man. I could eat a ham and cheese sandwich all day.

COACH: You're a revolting excuse for a man.

TEACHER: If there were a trust fund set up that's funded by a dollar donation each time a husband says to his wife *Get off my back*, I could pay off my student loan debt.

COACH: My wife says I should stop drinking coffee cuz of my heart arrythmia.

a poem found in a wallet lost at e.o. siecke state forest in call, texas

Spaghetti Man
There was a spaghetti man
on the side of the road.
His sign said *God Bless*
Anything Helps.
His hands shook.
Skin stuck to bones.
His jaw working as if he
were chewing rocks.
His nose was so long
it kept tapping his chin.
Like a dick on his face.
A dick he could smell me through.
When I caught his eye
I only saw a corpse.
Not a man.
I will see him again
in my nightmares.

The priest spoke: *And so she came back to the bakery after the gingerbread man had run away. She went to the baker and said "I want that gingerbread man" and the baker said "that'll be ten cents" and she said "you don't understand. he was mine. I made him" and the baker said "that'll be ten cents." So she paid him ten cents and the baker handed her the gingerbread man. This time, the gingerbread man didn't run away. She wrapped her fingers around him and said "I created you. I bought you. Now I own you." This is the principle that God wants for each of us. All we are to God is—*

The frail old white man sits in the back pew reaches next to him and puts his hand on his nurse's dark-skinned arm and says "You hear that. I own you." Later that day he takes her home and shows her the face of the Devil. She sits alone in church the following Sunday. The police find her later that day feeding pieces of him to the pigs out back of his house.

All she says is "Nice day if it doesn't rain."

in these terrible times
even the weather has anxiety

in a classroom at jasper high school

STUDENT: [pulls out gun from backpack]

TEACHER: [pulls out gun from hip holster]

STUDENT: [puts gun back in backpack]

TEACHER: [keeps gun pointed at student]

STUDENT: I hate math.

TEACHER: [fires]

in a classroom at jasper high school

BOY: Do you want to play house?

GIRL: Okay.

BOY: You goddamn bitch! Where's my mother fucking remote control?

GIRL: [starts crying]

TEACHER: Hang on. Do that again. The camera was out of focus.

**she asked people to not feel sorry for her when
she read this to her sixth grade class**

my mother made my bed before
she killed herself. she did
a sloppy job, bed making you do when you're in
a rush to get out the door.
it was the last nice thing she ever did
for me. she took
a handful of pills—little white dots spilled
onto the carpet. she laid
down for a nap and never left
the bed. she didn't leave
a note, but the bed making was enough:
i love you it said; *i'm sorry but i*
just can't do it anymore the sloppiness said;
i'm tired said her forever sleep.

**excerpt from a third grader's report on someone important
from history, found at jasper elementary**

Ed Gein sat on a throne of human skin. He ate Corn Flakes out
of a human skull. He kept his pants up with a belt of human
nipples stitched together with thread made from human hair. I
wonder if he did all this to feel like a person, because nothing
about him was human except for the skin he wore.

recording of this 40 year old dude i used to work with at the slaughterhouse in jasper, texas

Grampy telled me about how grammy die. Telled me bout this raffle at the cath-o-lick church when they's livin in Odessa. Grammy worked at the Waffle House. Grampy cut the meat off bucks people brung in to had stuffed. Now this raffle he telled me bout was only a buck and they fill this wheelbarrel up with whiskey and burbon and the like. Done this every year. Grampy telled me bout this old fella who done won it twice. He say that Grammy done quit when she don't win. Grampy put in a buck for her. He did it as a secret. That time he winned the wheelbarrell. Say it was Grammy's ticket that done won. So Grampy give her all them bottle. He couldn't wake her up the next day. He telled me this while his eyes were leakin.

TEACHER: Heredity is the passing of traits from parents to offspring.

GIRL: Like hair?

TEACHER: No. Like heart disease and alcoholism and depression.

BOY: Babies are made from sex.

TEACHER: Babies are usually made from depression and anxiety and the desire to have purpose outside of the self.

GIRL: My mommy's pregnant again. It's a boy.

TEACHER: Can anyone name something heredity will gift her new brother?

BOY: Hate?

TEACHER: Correct.

artwork collected from a second grader at jasper elementary

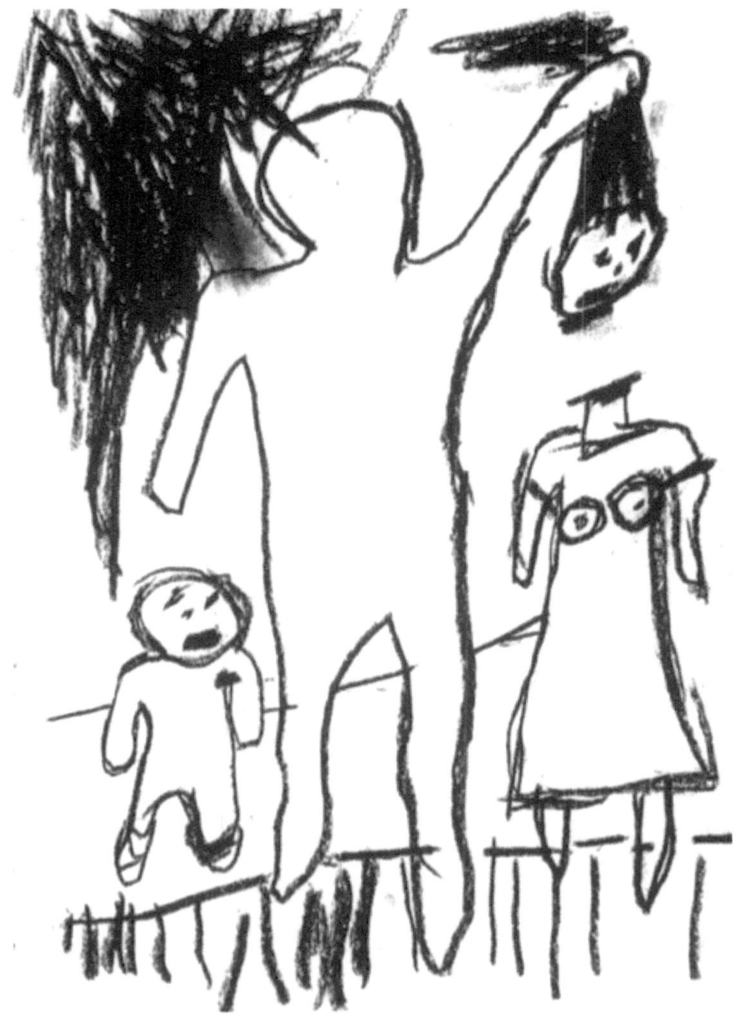

this is a memory i have from high school.

I had the prom queen disavowed. At the after party we walked in on her naked with three dudes banging each hole and three more dudes jacking off onto her. Snapped some pictures with my phone. They tore the title from her. She ended up switching schools. They did a report on the news about her. I heard she drowned herself in the mud of a pig pen. The principal kept the pictures. Hovered over them like a starving dog. They did a news report on him too. Wasn't the only pictures he had.

She awoke to the sound of her husband coughing. Distant. She found him in the garage, sitting in the running car. The garage was full of exhaust.

HUSBAND: Didn't want to wake you.

when there's nothing to do because there's nothing to do in jasper, texas

she got doped up on valium & passed out in the jack in the box drive-thru. she got doped up & passed out at the chinese restaurant with her senile grandparents, her brain damaged father, her sister, & her sister's gay boyfriend. her teeth fell out when she tried to eat caramel. the stickiness pulled them out of her gums. her mother burned alive. she used to fake being retarded so she could get money from people. her grandparents said she'd die before she turned nineteen. yesterday they buried her at the age of 21.

—To call back this number, press 7

—To save this message, press 8

—To delete this message because your mother has been dead for four years and these voicemails aren't going to bring you closer to her, press 9

—If you didn't know her in life and are trying to know her in death by listening to her vocal patterns in these voicemails, press the star key—the one that looks like a butthole.

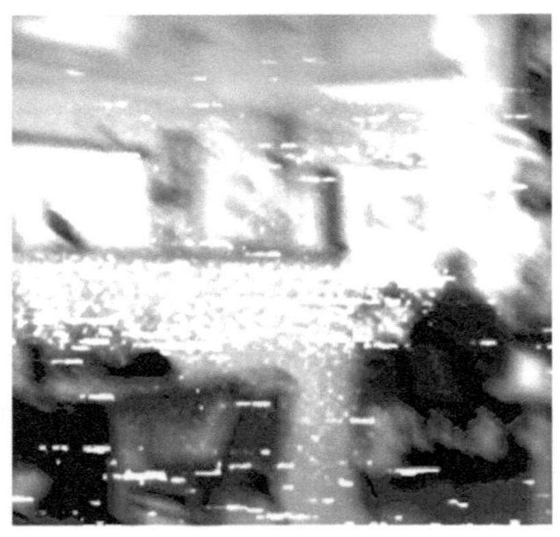

There's a guy who visits Ty's Diner in Jasper, Texas every day for lunch. People call him Prince, but he looks more like a jester. He's the kind of guy who thinks the best way to get rid of a booger is to eat it. He's the kind of guy who thinks dark comedy means movies like *Friday* or *Pootie Tang*. He works at the slaughterhouse and doesn't wear a mask. He used to drive around and give tramps Monopoly money. He always wears a shirt with a cartoon mouse on it and the mouse has a giant boner and it says *Here Kitty Kitty*. Someone told me he murdered his first wife by putting her head on the manifold of his F-150. This was back in 1964.

An old woman with the shakes pushes her liver & onions on the floor and screams *I don't care what happens to me, I just want to see someone get God out of office.*

mostly true
Swallowing a balloon full of drugs. He starts choking.
"What's wrong with you?"
The man starts screaming. "It popped."
"Man, why did you use water balloons?"
The man dies.

mostly true 2: the sequel
Swallowing a balloon full of hydrochloric acid & seltzer. He
starts choking.
"What's wrong with you?"
The clown starts screaming. "It popped."
"Man, why did you use balloon animal balloons?"
The clown dies.

give you the qualities of myself

my hands: once soft, now calloused, blistered. the hands of a dead
       whaler.

my heart: once an open sea, now beached, landlocked.

my future: once swollen with heavenly perfection, now a hare-lipped
       nightmare. sinking.

my drive: once a vessel plowing through every high wave, now a
       procrastinating—fuck it...

—today feels too much like the past

what she thought she could do to get out of jasper, texas

She does cam shows. She's six months pregnant. Men pay her more tips now. She masturbates while listening to Alan Watts speeches. She says things like *Spanking pregnant women is God's work*. Her armpit hair is longer than mine. She's the firework in Katy Perry's "Firework." She plans to have the baby live on webcam.

in a classroom at jasper high school

TEACHER: Can anyone tell me what their parents do for
      work?

STUDENT: My daddy sells salt.

TEACHER: What kind of salt?

STUDENT: He hangs his shoes outside.

TEACHER: Do you know your address?

STUDENT: [nods]

TEACHER: Can you write it down for me?

poem found in an abandoned backpack behind jasper elementary

The sheep are all in a row.

Throats cut open. Blood spurting.

Legs kicking in chaotic unison.

Knives hacking limbs, flaying flesh, tearing hide.

Nervous eyes of the young watch the mutilation of the old.

Chains pull corpses high off the ground.

Blood runs in rivers across steel grates

and cracked concrete. Fear and profits.

A return to the putrification of physical reality.

Necks and legs of the young snapped like dead wood.

Bile rises, boils over, spills out jagged useless holes.

Knives sharpen. A trade of flesh.

The machine grinds on.

this is funny.

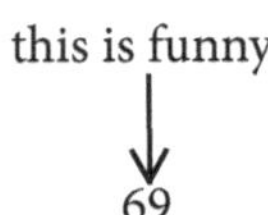

Suck you while spanking me, no scam - m4w (Jasper, TX)
looking for some rough sex, skull fuck me,
pound my boy pussy. Spank or whip this cross
dressing ass. tie my hands behind me. slap and
kick my cock and balls. Make fun of my little
dick and small balls. I have a wooden spoon if
you like you can beat my dick with because it's
so pathetic. share me with some of your friends.
I will be wearing a bra, nylons, garter belt, panties, slip, short skirt,
blouse. I cannot host. Livin w/ dying mother & stepson. looking
for jasper area only. Text me or call me if it's after 10 p.m. to wake
me up. call me bitch slut, baby

body: average

height: 6'3" (190cm)

status: divorced

age: 65

GUYS ON DATING APPS
*Hello, I just masturbated while watching you through your social
window. Can we make love?*

PEDOPHILES ON CRAIGSLIST
Give me your kiddies. I'm doing God's work.

a deep east texas craigslist ad in the rant and raves section

LOOKOUT! setting up stings (Jasper, TX)
State police setting up stings to catch us out here. BE CAREFUL!!
Fake ads, if the boy's name is Dallas or Derek or Matt and he sends
you a pic wearin his junior high sweater. Like that show, but no
cameras. Just police. Try Lufkin or Livingston.

the only thing that makes him smile

DAD: Most successes spring from failures.

SON: That sounds like a fortune cookie.

Dad crunches on a fortune cookie.

DAD: Interesting. Doesn't make it less true.

SON: Tell that to Ahab.

DAD: I try not to talk to Muslims.

happening right now in jasper, texas

A blind albino woman with a service dog walks down the sidewalk. It's almost noon. Heat shimmers like jet fuel. A child runs up to her dog and the child's mother says *Don't touch it*. The blind woman says *Hello*, but the mother and child are gone. Her dog stops next to a half-eaten chicken wing covered in maggots. The dog sniffs, coughs, then crams the chicken wing into its mouth. It tries to swallow, but the chicken wing doesn't move. The dog gags twice, then drops dead. The blind woman waits for her dog to keep moving. It never does. She stands alone in the heat, sun making blisters on her delicate skin. Cars pass. People pass and when she says *Help me* they say *I don't have any money*. At around four, she collapses, tongue swelling out of her mouth. An ambulance picks her up at six. In the hospital the next day, waking from a heat stroke-induced coma, the woman whispers *Where's Milky?* No one knows what she's talking about. They bring her six 25 cent milk cartons. A nurse stands by the bed and holds the milk carton so the blind woman can drink. There's a catalogue printed in braille so blind people can choose their service dogs. She finds one named *Pip*. No one knows about this because it hasn't been made into a movie yet.

a pastime in jasper, texas

The doctor told him to stop holding in his shit. *When you have to go, find a bathroom and go.* The doctor gave him a list of dangers, results of holding in shit, a list that peaked with death. He didn't stop holding in his shit. It felt too good. The pressure against his anus, in his intestines, the farts as they pushed past the backed-up shit. An ejaculation of the anus. That's the only way he could describe it. Prolonged pleasure. All of it building up to an explosion of ecstasy. His feces going black, intestines sucking out all nutrition, lumps of deadly toxins. He lives longer than the doctor. And happier.

BITCHY TEENAGER BITCHES

She's the type of person who uses the term "narrative" because she heard it in a Taylor Swift song. She once dated a guy who would go to magazine stands and tear out all the cologne ads so that he would never have to buy cologne. She had to clean out her mother's house after her mother died of an overdose. They found her mother half in her wheelchair, half on the bathroom floor. They say she was trying to get to the toilet to throw up the vicodin she swallowed.

BITCHY TEENAGER: This sucks.

how it is i know not, but i do know that in this ditch with these things spilling out from the bottom of the empty vessel where my soul should be, a chasm opening in me, i am nearing the end of my honeymoon phase with life. no longer a cozy, loving pair—sometimes the things we think taste terrible aren't terrible after we try a sample. i've speared a toothpick's worth, now i crave the whole catch. find it in the freezer aisle.

HOMAGE IS AN

steal everything

EXCUSE FOR

you can and own

UNORIGINAL

what you steal.

THOUGHT.

this is all homage.

at a doctor's office waiting room

NURSE

Stan?

GOTH

Dammit… I meant to write Satan.

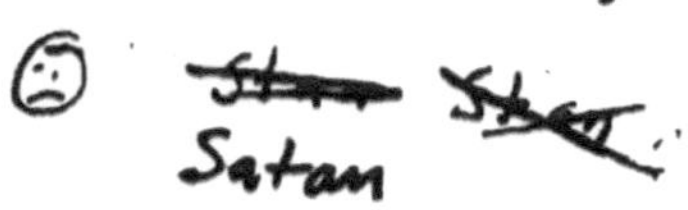

Freeballing at China Cafe – m4m (Tyler, TX) 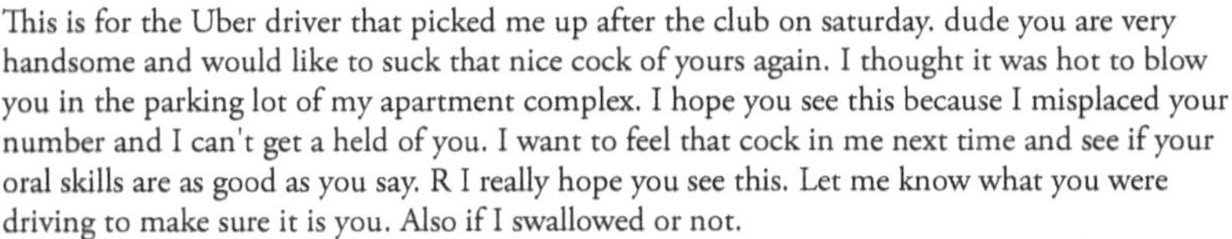

Ran into you at The China Cafe in Tyler Christmas Day. You were a white guy in black sweat/jogging pants freeballing. Your dick was bulging and i couldn't stop staring. You are by yourself and was quite friendly wishing me a Merry Christmas and asking where i was from. I stared at your cock the whole time you stood in front of me talking. I'd like to see those pants pulled down.

Looking for missing person(Kilgore)

My cousins is looking for his son about 250 lbs 6'2" he has down syndrome. Pleas have him call home if you see someone like him. Samoan light brown skin. pls, email if you see someone similar to this descriptions.

RE: suicide freak.

Tard...!!!!!!!!!!!!!!!!!!!!!!!!!!!!!!!!!!!!!!!

Wal Mart Livingston – w4m (Livingston, TX)

To the guy in Wal Mart in Livingston, at the self check out on Wednesday, January 3, 2018. You were paying out as I was walking in with my mom, she actually notice you starring at me and she mention it to me. I slowly turned around and made eye contact with you, I got shy and turned my head. I wish i would've smiled or said hi. If you remember me, confirmed with me what you were wearing and how you looked like so I know its you.

Very handsome hispanic Uber driver. – w4m (Beaumont, TX)

This is for the Uber driver that picked me up after the club on saturday. dude you are very handsome and would like to suck that nice cock of yours again. I thought it was hot to blow you in the parking lot of my apartment complex. I hope you see this because I misplaced your number and I can't get a held of you. I want to feel that cock in me next time and see if your oral skills are as good as you say. R I really hope you see this. Let me know what you were driving to make sure it is you. Also if I swallowed or not.

- do NOT contact me with unsolicited services or offers

re: tired (Unemployment Office)

How about learning the language that ONE-THIRD of Americans speak, like it or not? That makes you more marketable as a worker, *pendejo*

re: REVENGE (sexual encounters) – m4w (Pequod, TX)

I am a man of many humanities. A godly man. But I have my flaws. I crave quenchlessly the desire for revenge. I am looking for a boy. A large white boy. The greatest love of my life—but almost my deepest nightmare. I must find him. I need a crew of six men. WE'RE GOING TO HARPOON THE FAT SON OF A BITCH!

Dear Son,
My desire to know you has never died.
I've painted you somewhere in the Sistine
Chapel of my mind--

Dear Son,
This is something that happened to me
when I was twelve years old. I've found
it in here and the only way to keep it is
if I put it down for you to read--

Dear Son,
I know this is an impossibility so take
it as a not-so-subtle suggestion: don't
ever drink and don't ever inhale when
someone passes you a "cigarette" they
rolled themselves--

Dear Son,
I was arrested today. They say I struck a
child, a young girl. Slapped her in the
ear. But I have no recollection--

Dear Son,
You will born but I don't REMEMBEr it. Do you remember WEN I took you to the park and ALL U WANTED to do was play on the playground? Your MOMMY had agoraphobia. She NOT C UR 2 grade play.

DEER SAMEE,
WE ARE IS THE LIGHT. 12 FIV ON A CHAPEL. BE BE BOO BOO. OKAY?

EEEEEEEEEEEE30RQ,
SMILESDF. THIS STHIS THIS THIS THTIF THIF DTGFGOFD SDO SDJWLMMF.D..

he told everyone his brain was foggy cuz he drank too much wine. now he asks his son "who are you?" every time they see each other. soon he won't remember how to form words. then he'll die. dementia.

a diary found at a crime scene in jasper, texas

what does it mean if i'm aroused by the body of a naked man? what if i touch him? what if i lean in to kiss him & never pull back? what if i take him into me or i feel myself in him enveloped by the jungle heat of his mouth? what if this feels more true than all the fucking i've done? what would my god think of me? what happens when people—family friends strangers—call me *faggot* & try to convince me through hate & violence that this *choice* i've made is wrong & that *faggots* are the cause of this country being on the wrong track? what can i say when they tell me my love is just pure fucking trash? what will they say if they wake up & see an image of a member of their sex & find themselves hard or wet with the juices of lust and love? how many times has this already happened? how many times have they silenced this voice with a sledgehammer to the mouth? what would they think if they knew the depression never changes? what if i told them that the shame only becomes external? truth + denial + hate + love + acceptance + love + fear + me + you = _________

what is the answer to this equation?

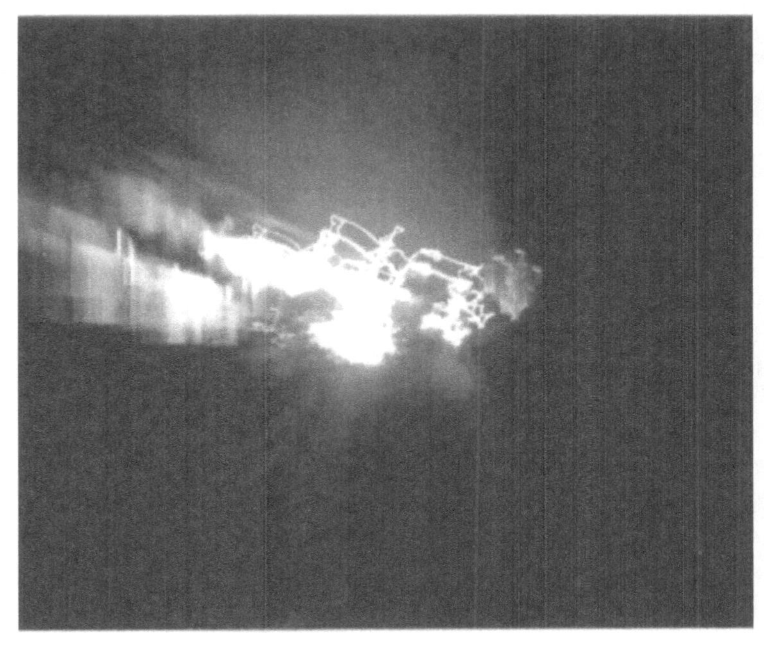

I meant to take your
picture but I fucked
it up

on a quiet street where old ghosts meet—
a friday night in jasper, texas

"Did you get your teeth fixed?"
"Nah, they're just mints."
Eats mints.

Girls dancing in the street:
"I'm never having kids."

At the counter of a Little Caesars:
"Order for Batman."
A black man steps up to counter.
"Yeah?"
"You're Batman?"
"Oh, I thought you said black man."
The black man steps back. Batman walks up and grabs his pizza.
"Order for bitch slut."

"We're young. We're free tonight to get loaded and do whatever
the hell we want."
"Does anyone have any Pepto chewables?"
"In the 80s, I used to be the mother fuckin sun."
"When I was 10, I was in love with my dog. He was my first kiss."

On the street corner:
An ice truck pulls up.
PEDESTRIAN: Hey, let's see that dead body you got in the back.
Driver of the truck gets out and beats pedestrian with a claw hammer.

art confiscated from a second grader at jasper elementary

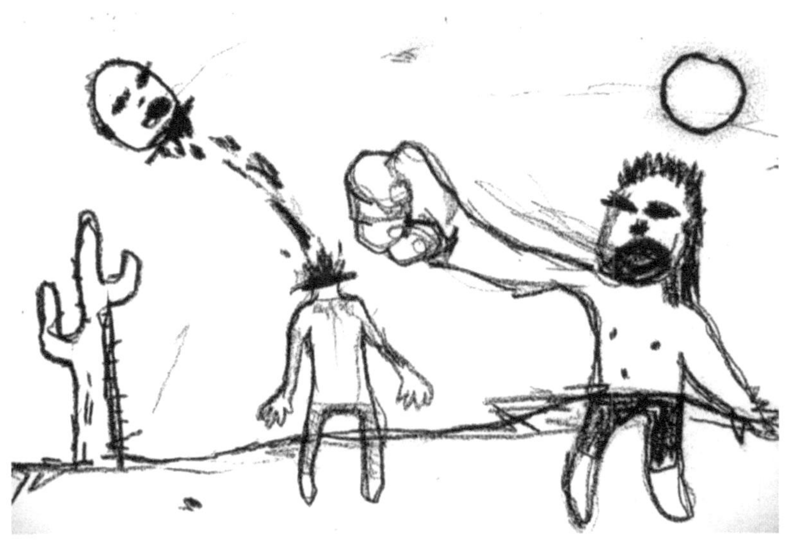

Her father beat her. Her teachers beat her. Her first boyfriend beat her. So did her third. Her first husband beat her. Her son, had he lived, would've probably beat her. She married a man with no arms. He gave her flowers with his feet. Short pink azaleas. The only time he laid his feet on her was when she'd get home from two shifts at the diner and he'd give her a back rub. They had a daughter. She was born with both arms. She never hit her mother. She learned to play the oboe. No one ever beat her again.

meaning is

———

important

He rented a studio apartment from a sex offender. He didn't know this at first. It wasn't until his third month living in the apartment when he awoke at 3:34am to find his landlord standing at the end of his bed. The landlord was naked, his cock going in and out of the gaps between his feet.

PequodPCS 6:66 PM 1%
Messages Rachel Details
i thought u would save me
not my problem
im afraid out here. alone.
ur obsessed. ur hunting for a reason to hate urself
ive already found it
i bought my coffin today
ok
can you return it?
Text Message Send

A person's thumb size is determined by the size of their momma's nipple. The nipple shapes the infant mouth & the infant shapes the thumb through sucking. Women with long nipples will raise astonishing hitchhikers.

in jasper, this is also how a baby's penis size is determined.

six white trash girls at the paradise trailer park in jasper, tx

Two are doing hopscotch while the other four double dutch. All the girls chant:

chip off the old block
slip on a young cock
bun in the oven
& brisket on the roast
spread butter on your cheeks
& jelly on your toast
daddy left for smokes
got some gas to burn a cross
criss criss cross criss cross
 1 3 5 7
none of us will go to heaven
& if you do not like it
then you can go to
hello
goodbye
all of us
are gonna die

You take your time getting ready. Wash your hair, body, face, genitals. You dress your-self in new clothes. Almost perfect. But in the mirror you see a zit, pregnant with a little white head—tight & shiny. Real casual you put fingers on either side, try & push those fingers together. You've got two hours until they give away your reserva-tion at that restaurant everyone's going to, where they serve meals in troughs. Two hours…plenty of time to coif your hair, drive to your date's place, get gas & flowers on the way, compliment your date & drive to that restaurant before they give away your reservation. So you push your fingers together and punish the whitehead on your relatively blemish-free face. There's a pressure that reminds you of the dentist. And the closer your fingers get to each other, the more that spot on your face feels like that one time you had to get a double root canal and the anesthesia wore off too soon. Your eyes water. Blood rushing to your face makes your skin turn the same shade of red as the zit. And just when you think you can't take it, that you'll just give up & go on your date with a zit so big it'll need to introduce itself, there's this soul-pulling thunk as the two index fingers meet and the pregnant whitehead crowns & gives birth. A line of cotton-colored ooze spits out and connects your face to the mirror. It's a magnificent eruption. And in this moment that feels better than any orgasm, you know you will wake every day hoping for another zit on your face. But you stop thinking about how this situation feels because you notice that this tightrope of pus is silly-stringing from your face in a near-constant stream, collecting shampoo-in-palm on the mirror, covering your reflection, white drops spattering the wall, the sink, your toothbrush, everything. You think of your date and wonder if anything like this has ever happened to them. Your index fingers move away from the zit, but the geyser of pus continues to erupt. The feel-goodness turns to fatigue. There's this scooping in your toes, spreading up your feet, ankles. When it reaches your calves you notice that the pus has swallowed the mirror, filled the sink, overflowed onto the floor, slowly flooding the bathroom. The sound of the still-flowing stream is similar to the fart of a half-empty ketchup bottle. That scooping moves up past your knees and into your thighs. When you look down, the stream waterhosing in whatever direction you turn your head, you notice that your legs have crumpled like an empty chip bag. When you try & move your legs, you can't. You're now ankle-deep in pus and the scooping moves past your freshly cleansed genitals and into your stomach, where you see your stomach crumple, everything inside gone. This scooping creeps into your heart and the zit goes all Mount St. Helens, exploding creamy pus all over the room, collecting in the corners, slathering the walls, coating the only window in the bathroom. The pus has pushed the door shut and you know getting it open will be impossible. You're trapped. But you don't care because the way it scoops at your heart & the way your heart explodes, an explosion that makes you think of your date, who you hope waits for you with the same violently pleasant excitement, this scooping feels as if your life has been leading up to this moment and only this. Your body is warmed by the zit muck, which now covers you, crawling up your neck, over your chin, up over your mouth, which is where the scooping is now. All you can hear is an underwater gurgle as the pus spurts continuously from your face. You don't pay attention to your breath, the pus keeping you from finding it. Cream takes over your vision and you're nowhere, floating embryonic in a room filled with pus. You don't think about how you can't breathe, about how out of all the ways you've envisioned yourself slipping into the Big Quiet drowning in zit juice was never one of them. What you do think about is your date, who will hear that you died & that responders pumped gallons of zit pus out of you & your bathroom. Your date will always remember you as that person with the zit pus—even though what was inside you could've been called love if the feeling could be reduced to such a simple word.

LOCKED ROOM MYSTERY

On the twenty first day in the room, he knew he would never escape. So he gave up.

<u>THE END</u>

since i've already stolen so much from so little, i'll
leave this here with a final theft. i don't care. do you?

texas, texas: from hell's heart i stab; for hate's sake i spit
fuck you—you blackest gorge, you hollowed-out skull
filled with woe & madness
rage & hate dealt by this whole
state i burst my hot heart's shell upon it
i want to forgive your cursed nature
but i don't care enough
the savagery has infected me, my heart's hate pointed
inward now, out of your guilt
so sink, sink, & have mercy on those you pull
into the depths of your living coffin

3.
scenes from a partially unproduced film about his life titled:
hummingbird

INT. STORAGE FACILITY

Inside the unit where Ishmael Dick lives. He puts a VHS tape in a half-burnt VCR. The TV plays static images of a family opening presents on Christmas morning. The timestamp reads **12/25/1989**.

Ishmael gets in bed, naked.

SON (ON TV): This is exactly what I wanted.

He falls asleep while a family that isn't his enjoy their happiness.

INT. STORAGE FACILITY

Ishmael wakes up inside his unit—a bedroll on the floor, a table, a chair, a TV, a bunch of VHS tapes, a VCR. The rest of the unit is filled with junk, trash, booze bottles.

He gets up, prepares for the day: puts on a wrinkled suit, fixes his hair, picks up a length of rope, ties it into a noose, wraps the noose around a pipe sticking out of the ceiling.

He stands on the chair, eases the noose around his neck, pins a note to his shirt. A deep breath. He steps off the chair.

SNAP!

The pipe breaks. Ishmael crashes down onto the table. It collapses under his weight, and he rolls onto the floor. Water spews from the broken pipe. He lies in a pile of cracked, splintered wood, water raining down, pooling around him. All his stuff—wet and ruined.

ISHMAEL: another day.

EXT. COLLEGE CAMPUS

At a bulletin board filled with flyers. Ishmael reads one.

FLYER: Attention—A research study group is conducting a clinical trial regarding sprained muscles and a potential local anesthetic. If you have sprained your ankle in the last three days and would like to participate in the study, come to the Daniel Plainview Memorial Center, Room 82 between 4pm and 6pm. All accepted applicants for the study will receive a $200 compensation.

Ishmael jumps from various spots, attempting to sprain his ankle. He jumps, lands wrong and something snaps. He screams.

INT. ROOM 82

A Grad Student Nurse checks his ankle. It's purple & gross. She presses. There's a crunch.

NURSE: This is broken. You need to go to a hospital.

ISHMAEL: can i participate?

NURSE: This is broken.

ISHMAEL: does that qualify me for the $200?

NURSE: You need to go to a hospital.

ISHMAEL: you do.

He limps out.

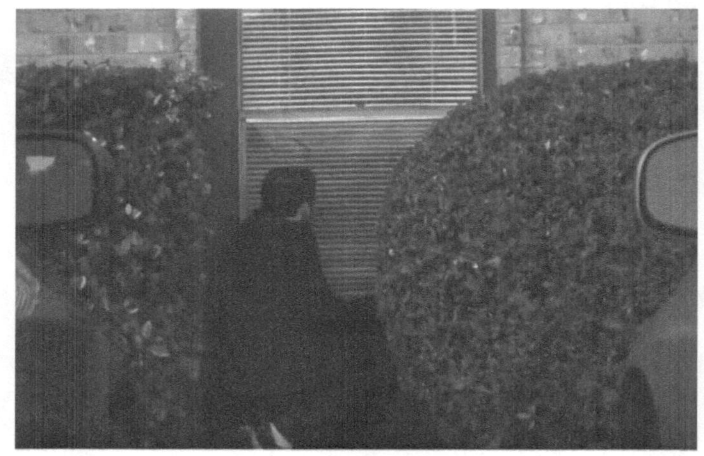

Ishmael spies on other people's lives.

INT. STORE

Ishmael walks in. Two Workers standing nearby, one preparing to mop the bathrooms, quietly mock him.

WORKER 1: (get a load of this guy. look at that haircut.)

WORKER 2: (look at his fuckin suit. he looks like a fuckin hobo.)

WORKER 1: (he's probably a homo.)

Ishmael eases past them and enters the bathroom.

INT. BATHROOM

Ishmael's pissing against the wall between two urinals. It sprays everywhere. He shakes it off, zips, and turns around. Some Dude's taking a shit with the door open.

SHITTER: Yo man.

Ishmael nods.

SHITTER: I think I recognize you. You work at that Waffle House next to Chuck E Cheese?

ISHMAEL: no

SHITTER: I used to go to that Waffle House but now I can't go within 1000 feet of a Chuck E Cheese. And that Waffle House is 878 feet away. Had my stepdaughter count them.

ISHMAEL: mmmm

SHITTER: Did you know that when he was in Texas,
    Conway Twitty would only eat at Waffle House?

ISHMAEL: mmmm

SHITTER: Would you be a sweetheart and see if the next stall
    has t.p.? I'm fresh out.

Ishmael looks. There's a full roll.

ISHMAEL: it's out too.

SHITTER: Fucky.

ISHMAEL: you're wearing socks. use em.

He walks out.

INT. STORE

As he passes the Workers—

ISHMAEL: someone pissed all over the wall, all over the floor.
    it's a mess.

WORKER 1: Was it you?

ISHMAEL: sorry, i'm deaf.

He walks off.

In an aisle: Ishmael's compares two cough syrups, then after what appears to be a concerned internal debate, he rips open both boxes. Shoves the bottles in his jacket.

Another aisle: He drinks a Yoo-Hoo. Spits it out. Puts it back on the shelf, half empty.

Another aisle: he takes a magazine off the rack. Opens to a scented cologne ad. Tears it out. Shoves it in his pocket. Grabs another magazine, does the same thing. His pockets fill with cologne ads.

*He picks up a book—***MOBY DICK***. He flips through it. Stops somewhere near the end. Reads a passage loud as hell.*

ISHMAEL: ...and in conclusion, Ahab buttfucked a vat of blubber and sucked off a spear crusty with cum and piss and went back home to Texas and raised seventeen illegitimate children by six different wives and opened a church near the swamp and lived happily ever—

Then the Shitter walks up.

SHITTER: You're a fucking dick.

ISHMAEL: ok

The Shitter walks off, bare feet squeaking in his shoes. Then, over the store PA—

VOICE: Ishmael...uh...Zitty, your prescription's ready.

Ishmael drops the book, walks off.

AT THE PHARMACIST'S COUNTER

Ishmael tries to grab the prescription. The Pharmacist pulls it back.

PHARMACIST: Now you're gonna wanna take these with lots of water. And whatever you do, don't drink. Some people have been known to like freak out. Like there was this one guy who took these and had a beer, just one beer, and the fire department had to get him out of a tree like a cat. Said he was arguing with himself. Like having two separate conversations. Using different voices and everything. Isn't that weird?

ISHMAEL: i think i can handle myself.

But she's no longer paying attention to him. Texting.

ISHMAEL: i'm gonna steal all this stuff now.

PHARMACIST: ...hmmm?

She's still not paying attention. So he walks off. After a beat—

PHARMACIST: Wait...he didn't— Did he pay?

EXT. ALLEY

A group of PRE-TEEN BOYS talk hard and gesture like thugs. Cigarettes in each's hand. They don't even have dick hair yet.

PRE-TEEN 1: And she said, "But you're fucking some girl from another school." And I said, "Shut up, bitch. I was fuckin ya mama last night."

The other Pre-teens laugh. Ishmael approaches.

ISHMAEL: freeze, police. you boys old enough to smoke those? let me see some i.d. … nah, i'm kidding. gimme one of those.

A shocked Pre-teen gives him a cigarette.

ISHMAEL: you idiots are smoking the good stuff. what'd you pay for a pack of these? seven, eight bucks?

PRE-TEEN 2: Huh?

ISHMAEL: these. things. will. kill. you. you are all being fucked over by a company that wants you dead. you stupid fuckers are paying someone to kill you. least you can do is not pay so damn much. get some chesters or sixers. three a pack. kill yourself twice as fast.

Ishmael takes a drag.

PRE-TEEN 1: But you're smoking too.

ISHMAEL: yes, i am. when you get to be my age, you learn
that life is a pile of rancid shit you're force fed. you get
to be my age, all you'll want to do is not live.

PRE-TEEN 1: How old are you?

PRE-TEEN 2: Man, that's sad.

ISHMAEL: yeah? sad? how 'bout i come over there and beat
your head in?

*He comes at the Pre-teens. But he's no match. They all whoop up
on him.*

ISHMAEL: i just pissed! i just pissed myself!!

EXT. HOUSE - NIGHT

NIGHTSHOT VIA SONY HANDYCAM—POV
Ishmael sneaks around the side of the house, breaks in.

INT. HOUSE

NIGHTSHOT VIA SONY HANDYCAM—POV
Ishmael walks through the house. Down a hallway. Past family photos hung on the wall.

He walks into the living room. Finds the TV. Opens cabinets around the TV until he finds one filled with VHS tapes. He digs through them. Finds one marked **FAMILY VACATION 1992**. *He puts it in his pocket.*

He goes to the kitchen. Opens the refrigerator. Digs through. Grabs some lunch meat. Finds the bread. Makes himself a sandwich. He puts nothing back.

He stands at the base of the stairs, looking at more family photos as he eats the sandwich he's made. A light goes on upstairs.

MAN'S VOICE: Who's down there?

ISHMAEL: …no one ….shit….uh….

MAN'S VOICE: Ishmael?

ISHMAEL: nothing!

Ishmael runs out of the house.

INT. STATE HOSPITAL

Ishmael, in the office of the Intake Doctor. An Orderly stands guard by the door.

INTAKE DOCTOR: If I asked your friends, how would they describe you...as a person?

ISHMAEL: ...oh, uh...real well...real good.

INTAKE DOCTOR: I'm afraid I don't follow.

ISHMAEL: they'd say: he's a real good guy.

INTAKE DOCTOR: And why do you think they would say that?

ISHMAEL: why wouldn't they say that?

INTAKE DOCTOR: I don't know. I don't know you.

ISHMAEL: i don't have any friends.

INTAKE DOCTOR: Then maybe people you know. Common people.

ISHMAEL: common people? like everyone?

INTAKE DOCTOR: ... Why do you want to stay here?

ISHMAEL: i am not me. i don't feel like i'm doing what should be. i don't know how other people are.

INTAKE DOCTOR: What do you want to do?

ISHMAEL: make money. get above...all this shit...all this stuff. maybe die. i don't know.

INTAKE DOCTOR: No, I mean, what do you want to do? What kind of career do you want to have?

ISHMAEL: i don't know. nothing.

INTAKE DOCTOR: Why wear the suit?

Ishmael shrugs.

INTAKE DOCTOR: When was the last time you had a job?

ISHMAEL: there was a time there where i...couldn't handle it.

INTAKE DOCTOR: Handle what?

ISHMAEL: working.

INTAKE DOCTOR: You couldn't handle working?

Ishmael nods.

INTAKE DOCTOR: ... how old are you, Ishmaellin?

ISHMAEL: thirty f— why does that matter?

INTAKE DOCTOR: Because I'm sitting here, looking at you, and I see someone who's lost his way, and is sadly losing his way back to the path every day.

ISHMAEL: the path?

INTAKE DOCTOR: You need to find a place, Ishmaellin. This world is so wild that we all must find our little places to fit...otherwise we'd...go, well, insane.

ISHMAEL: alright

INTAKE DOCTOR: Even animals have their purpose, have their own little place in this wild world. I'm looking at you. You're not mentally unstable. You don't need to be here. You're just lazy.

Ishmael leans across the desk.

ISHMAEL: how about you stop talking to me like i'm some fuckin moron before i shove this pen up your—

The Orderly lunges across the room, grabs Ishmael by his collar, shoves him onto the desk. Ishmael pushes off and the struggle gets violent. Clothes torn. Broken nose. Blood.

EXT. STREET

A Religious Pamphleteer on a street corner. Sandwichboard about god, sinners, & damnation hangs from his front and back.

RELIGIOUS PAMPHLETEER: Warm up to the love of the Lord. Let His warm Embrace save your eternal soul. Sir, have you found the love of the Lord? Did you know that Jesus Christ died 2,000 years ago for your sins, so that you wouldn't have to suffer for eternity? Isn't that something?

Ishmael walks up. Nose stuffed with bloody gauze. Eyes bruised. He reaches in this jacket. Pulls out some pamphlets.

ISHMAEL: can't believe they got us workin the same corner.

RELIGIOUS PAMPHLETEER: Excuse me?

Ishmael starts waving his pamphlets in the air.

ISHMAEL: the dark lord satan wants you to embrace your fellow human. not out of sin or fear, but out of pure desire and lust. we are all primitive beings and deserve the pleasures of our short time. embrace—

RELIGIOUS PAMPHLETEER: No! I am not with him! I am with the Lord! May God save his soul!

Ishmael stops shouting, walks over to the Pamphleteer.

RELIGIOUS PAMPHLETEER: Stay away from me!

ISHMAEL: hey man, i don't like that they put us here on the
    same day anymore than you do.

RELIGIOUS PAMPHLETEER: Who is they?

*A group of people walk up, look at Ishmael and the Pamphleteer.
Ishmael looks at them, at the Pamphleteer, and—*

ISHMAEL: no i will not let you smell my anus. (*to the group
    of people*) you hear that? this guy wants to smell my
    anus.

RELIGIOUS PAMPHLETEER: I never said that!

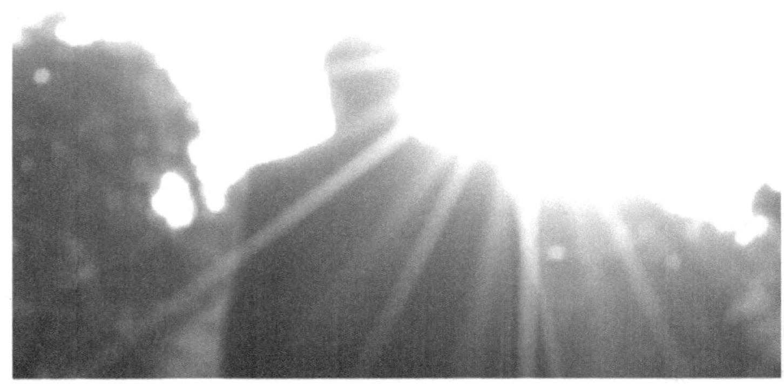

He turned his back on the world and found the light.

EXT. HIGHWAY 71

Ishmael walks along. Keeps to himself. A car pulls up. Driver (good ol boy) rolls down his window.

DRIVER: Lookin for a ride?

Ishmael doesn't answer.

DRIVER: I said you lookin for a ride fella?

Ishmael looks over at him.

DRIVER: You speaka English?

Ishmael nods.

DRIVER: Well you lookin for a ride?

ISHMAEL: no

DRIVER: Well where you walkin to? Ain't nothin around
          here.

ISHMAEL: just walking

DRIVER: Well where'd you come from? Ain't nothin around
          here. Closest town's about four hours walkin.

Ishmael doesn't answer.

DRIVER: Well surely you must need a ride.

ISHMAEL: i don't need any help.

DRIVER: Ain't no trouble. Headin to town anyway. You can even jump in the back if you don't feel safe. But I'm just a regular fella, ain't hurt a fly.

ISHMAEL: i don't need the fuckin ride you goddamn hillbilly.

DRIVER: What'd you say, fella?

Ishmael turns & runs into the woods to get away from the guy. Ishmael hides behind some bushes. Silence for a beat then—

DRIVER: I can still see you. ... behind that mesquite bush. What the hell're you doin? ... I can still see you.

ISHMAEL: no you can't.

DRIVER: Well, uh, yes I can. Right there between them two oaks. Got your foot stuck in a pile of deer shit.

ISHMAEL: no i don't.

DRIVER: Well what the hell're you doin?

Ishmael doesn't answer.

DRIVER: Forget it. Don't know what the hell the world's comin to when a man can't offer a stranded fella—

The car drives off. Ishmael steps out of the woods and starts walking in the opposite direction.

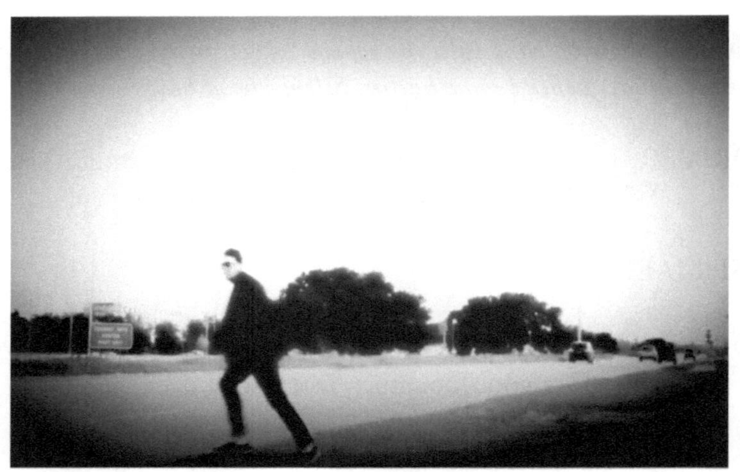

Ishmael crosses the highway.

EXT. WOODS (NEAR CREEK)

Ishmael beats the absolue shit out of an frail, elderly Fisherman. Brutal. Primitive. Then Ishmael digs through the unconscious man's things. Wallet...keys...fishing gear... Then—

Ishmael uses the stolen fishing gear...catches a fish...uses a rock to beat it to death...guts it...cleans it...cooks it...eats it.

JUST OUTSIDE THE WOODS

as Ishmael emerges from the wilderness and into a public park.

EXT. SMALL HOUSE

Ishmaels peeps through the window. Empty. Ishmael looks at the stolen I.D. and keys. Looks at the front door.

INT. SMALL HOUSE

as Ishmael snoops around, grabbing random items of worth, some useless junk. A kitten nuzzles his leg. Ishmael grabs the cat.

INT. PAWNSHOP

Ishmael sets the stuff on the counter.

PAWN MAN: Thirty-five

ISHMAEL: fifty

PAWN MAN: Thirty

ISHMAEL: fifty or i'll kill this cat.

PAWN MAN: Fifty then, you sick fuck.

Money on the counter.

ISHMAEL: know anyone that wants to buy a cat?

EXT. STREET

Ishmael walking, cat tucked under his arm. At the corner—

WOMAN: Aww, what an adorable kitty. What's its name?

ISHMAEL: you want it?

WOMAN: What?

ISHMAEL: you want to buy it for forty bucks?

WOMAN: N-no… that's all right.

She walks away, Ishmael stands. Moves to put his cigarette out on the cat but doesn't.

ISHMAEL (V.O.): i'm doing good. real good…things are.. things are picking up…

INT. STORAGE UNIT

Surrounded by trash. Boxes. Old food. Empty beer bottle. Ishmael smokes a cigarette, talks on the phone. It's an old rotary phone.

ISHMAEL: ...work is good, mom. ...yeah, i'm making some friends...we're going out tonight...i was thinking about getting a cat...no...yeah, but i was a kid then. kids don't take care of pets...i understand...hey, listen: do you think you and dad could loan me some— i know but i'm still waiting for that money to come in, and once it does, i'll be able to pay you back...i'll get a paycheck soon...they had something messed up...yeah...i miss you too...did i what?...someone broke in your house?...

He hangs up, lights a cigarette. The cat rubs its face against the hand holding the cigarette.

Focusing on the phone, the camera follows the cord down to the wall. There isn't a phone jack. The cord sits, unplugged.

EXT. STRIP MALL

Ishmael sneaks out from behind a dumpster, creeps over to a car, tries the lock. It's open. He sees a Suspicious Man come around the corner, sunglasses on. Ishmael gets in, hides.

INT. CAR

The Man ducks around a corner. Ishmael hotwires the car. He sits up and the Suspicious Man is there, standing next to a truck in the spot in front of the car Ishmael's in. Ishmael stays down.

The Man gets in the truck. Ishmael relaxes.

Thinking no one's watching, the Man digs a bra out of a shopping bag and tries it on, makes kissing faces at his rearview mirror.

Ishmael honks, scares the guy. They look at each other, the Man still holding the bra. Ishmael waves and drives off.

He opens the glove compartment. There's a gun inside.

EXT. RIVER

*Ishmael floats on a homemade raft. He drifts past two Homeless
Men taking baths in the river. One stands knee deep.*

HOMELESS MAN: Gets a little fast up there. You wanna be
        careful.

Ishmael says nothing.

HOMELESS MAN: Where ya headin?

ISHMAEL: towards death.

HOMELESS MAN: Have a safe journey.

*Ishmael puts some cash and food on two plates, sets them in the
water. They float toward the men.*

The Homeless Men watch Ishmael drift away.

EXT. RIVER – DUSK

Ishmael pulls his makeshift raft ashore. There's a guy sitting near a campfire, alone. He's reading **MOBY DICK**.

LONER: don't fuck with me, man. if you're coming to fuck
      with me, just don't.

Ishmael walks up to the fire, warms himself.

ISHMAEL: i'm hungry.

Loner keeps reading. Ishmael sits.

LONER: i don't have any food.

ISHMAEL: what're you doing out here?

LONER: do you ever have a moment where you feel like your
      life is adding up to something?

ISHMAEL: almost never.

LONER: where you feel like your life's about to add up to
    something, that the energy you've been waiting for,
    the energy that's going to change you and make you
    the person you think you were always destined to be,
    is here and you feel this rush of purpose and you feel
    ok with everything, and then in the same breath you
    realize how fucking wrong that is and you feel more
    worthless, hopeless, and pathetic than you did before?

ISHMAEL: shut the fuck up, please.

LONER: you remind me of someone.

Ishmael pulls out a gun and shoots himself in the mouth.

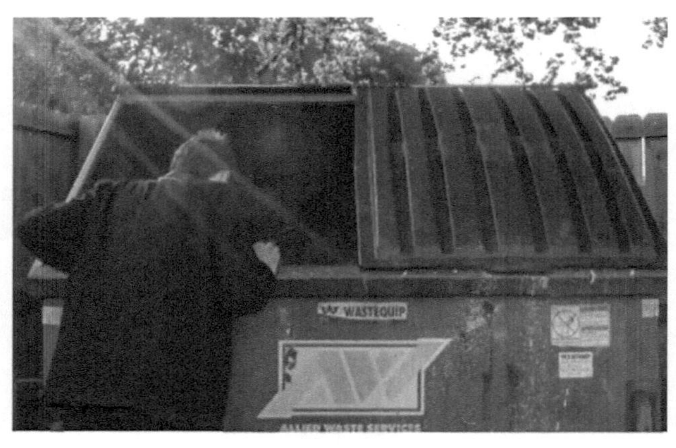

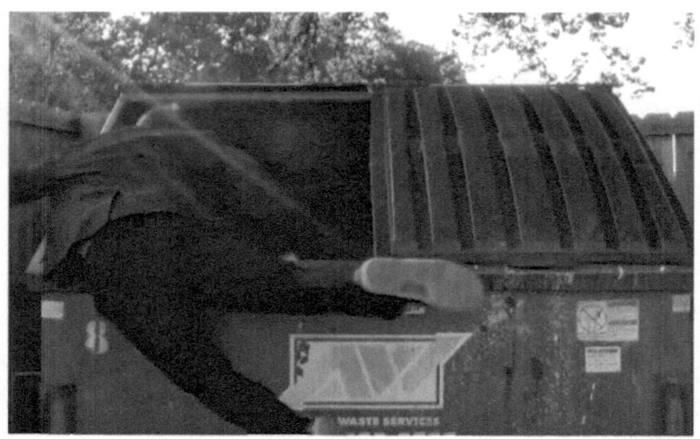

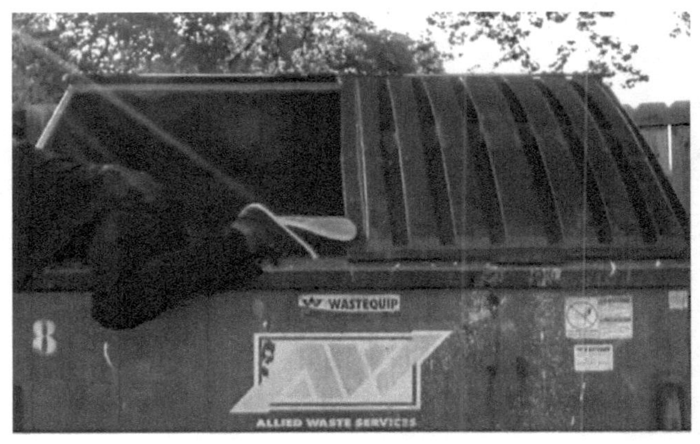
WASTEQUIP
ALLIED WASTE SERVICES
8

The following was found among the personal effects of an unknown man—whose body was recovered from Trout Creek in the E O Siecke State Forest near Call, TX. He had been dead almost two weeks. A mother and her three 8yo boys stumbled upon him. His body was covered with mosquitos. Though there was no note, sufficient evidence led authorities to believe he died from a combination of self-inflicted starvation & toxic levels of cough syrup. These are his final words. They have not been altered. No one has claimed his body. There is no next of kin. Today's his 35th birthday. This is mostly true.

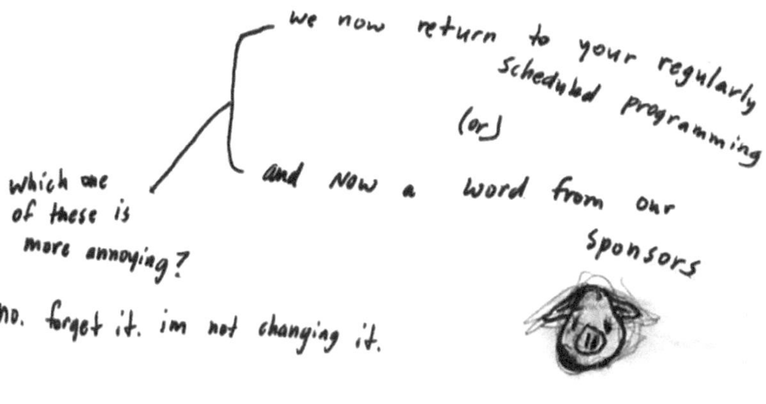

ACKNOWLEDGMENTS

Valorie: You're the bravest woman I've ever met. Thank you for letting me love you. **SPM**: Thank you for sending me on the whale hunt, ye masterful harpooneer. **to this other guy i know who also read it**: i made the turn <3. **To everyone who read this book at some point**: You the real ones. Let's party.

A big ol' whale of a **HECK YEAH** goes to Andersen Prunty for taking this hideous beast and giving it a home.

And many thanks to the editors who published pieces from this book—*Expat Press, Fiction International,* and *Permafrost.*

ABOUT THE AUTHOR

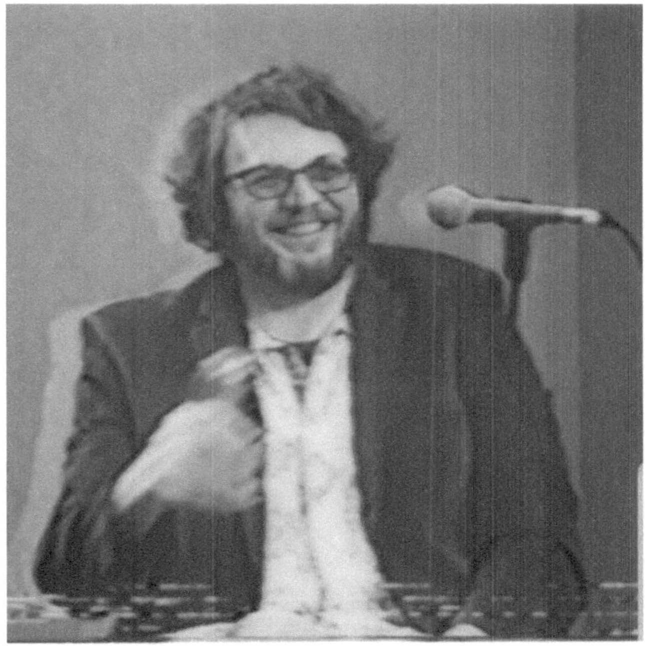

TEX GRESHAM was born & raised in Texas. He lived in California for a minute—it was nice. His work has been published in *Hobart*, *F(r)iction*, *The Normal School*, *Back Patio Press*, and *Booth*, among other places. [Insert a witty & quirky fake factoid about self] LOL! Can you believe it? Anywho... He lives in Las Vegas with his partner and kid. He tweets mostly nonesense from @thatsqueakypig.

www.squeakypig.com